THE Tool Box

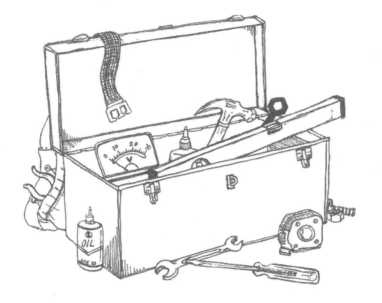

Building Better Relationships with Teens

Karren J Garrity MS, LPC, NCC
Individual and Family Therapy

ISBN-10: 0615640427
ISBN-13: 978-0-615-64042-6

Printed and bound in the United States

Editing by Joanne Shwed (www.AuthorOneStop.com)

Cover/interior design and production by Joanne Shwed, Backspace Ink (www.backspaceink.com)

Illustrations by Lee Ellen Sohl

To order copies: https://www.createspace.com/3705445

Amazing!

I am so grateful for the support and encouragement from my family and friends.

Mom, for all of those initial edits, you helped me launch this project.

Cathe, for your clearheaded read-throughs and the assurance that what I am saying makes sense.

Ruth, for your pure "Ruth-ness," you were absolutely worth waiting for!

Roxanne, you said, "Go for it, Ma," and I did.

Rachel, for your enthusiasm and thoughtful responses (as always) that helped me find the right words.

Hazel, for the assistance with dialogs so I wouldn't embarrass myself (or you!).

Chris, for being The Guy, believing in me and this project. You are my rock.

To the others who have bolstered me along the way: Sarah, Pat, Harriet, Moira, Darlene, Judy, Ajia, and Kathleen. Your interest and enthusiasm are invaluable to me.

Thanking you all.

Contents

PART I

Is This Book for You?

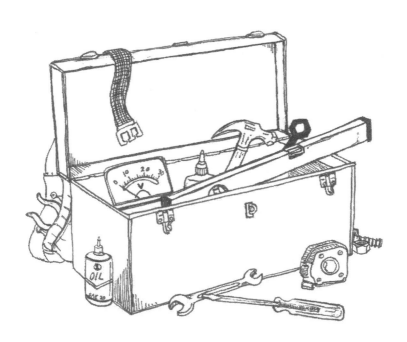

CHAPTER 1

Let's Get Started

Imagine These Scenarios

Life has been pretty normal for the Judson family. They have two daughters: Elizabeth is in college and Rebecca is a sophomore in high school. So far, things have gone well. Both girls have been honor students and each has had friends whom the parents have enjoyed. Elizabeth is an athlete and Rebecca loves to play the cello.

Starting a few months ago, however, the parents began to worry about Rebecca. It became apparent that she had been lying about where she was going and with whom she was spending time. She has also ignored her curfew for the past three weekends. The Judsons never had these problems with Elizabeth.

Meanwhile, in the Miller family, a shouting match between Dad and daughter Susan once again ended with her angrily storming off. Moments afterward, a frustrated Dad recalled his high-school days, and realized that he was beginning to sound just like his own father had. He remembered how he hated fighting with his dad, and how he had sworn that he would not be inflexible and closed-minded with his children. Dad would like to do things differently.

The Tool Box is designed for use with mainstream teenage scenarios. All families have times when everyday life feels overwhelming and, when that family has a teenager in the picture, stress can be high. This hands-on, easy-to-understand book will provide a variety of strategies and specific tools to help parents communicate with and nourish teenagers.

This is an action-oriented reference guide, a "how-to" manual for people whose children have become, or are about to become, teenagers. The chapters offer new skills to apply to various situations, including discipline, communication, negotiation, compromise, trust, tips for self-esteem, peer pressure, basic coping skills, money issues, and physical activity. It will be helpful for those who are already wading through difficult issues as well as for those who want to enter this phase with new tools in hand.

Kids today live in a very complicated world, and raising them is more complex than ever before. Gathering a lot of theory or devoting time to too much study will not help us be successful with the spontaneous interactions in which we often find ourselves with young people. *The Tool Box* provides a variety of strategies and specific tools, coaching adults who live and work with adolescents, so the adults survive and the kids thrive.

How to Use This Book

Read this book in a time of calmness. It is helpful to become familiar with the tools when we are not amidst a stressful situation. Plan to revisit it often. Some ideas and concepts hold current interest and some will be more appealing than others. Place a mark in the margin, circle an idea, or dog-ear a page. If it seems like a good idea to try a certain tool right away, *go for it*. Try using one or two tools. Remember to go back to the book when something feels off target. Each time a chapter is reread, it may offer a new insight.

Raising our children is an ongoing process because our kids change, the world changes, and we change, too. What did not work last month might work this month. Emotional, social, and financial stressors are a huge part of our culture. Influences that did not even exist 10 or 15 years ago affect our families today.

The Tool Box understands that parenting is a constantly evolving process, and it has been designed with this in mind. Treat the contents of this book as a collection of tools. All of the ideas are easy to understand and simple to use. Find five likeable tools, try three, and discover one that works!

Why This Book Helps

The Tool Box is for first-time parents as well as for seasoned mommas and poppas. For day-to-day living, many caregivers—including parents, grandparents, and even teachers—need simple ways of doing difficult things.

Parents may feel perplexed by certain issues, such as a teen's escalating social life and the need for curfews, worldly consequences as well as personal ones, self-respect, and respect for authority. These challenges are not very different for the seasoned parent or the veteran teacher, who has tried *everything*! Each child is unique, each community offers its own challenges, and each stage of our own lives brings specific issues. This book is helpful for these varied circumstances.

For example, just because the sink has clogged up—*again*—it does not mean the same thing is clogging it or that the optimal method used to unclog it will be the same. If there is a construction project, and we go to the hardware store to pick up some nails or screws, we may have to try a few before we get the one that will fit the job the best. Likewise, I have spent years collecting techniques, trying them in various situations to see which ones work where and why, and discarding those that don't.

The goal of *The Tool Box* is to share these tools with adults and their kids so that families can work *together*, with a try-one-on-for-size, *solution-focused* approach. In the process, parents—and children—will establish clearer ways to talk with each other.

Sometimes we need a little help to get through a sticky situation with our kids. What works for one child might not work for their sibling, and what worked when that child was 15 won't necessarily work when they're 16.

Perhaps we feel cornered and cannot seem to find our way out. We may realize that what we are doing is not working and want to try something different. *The Tool Box* will provide specific skills for difficult situations and show how to:

- Communicate effectively.

- Identify core issues.

- Be better able to prioritize needs and wants.

- Navigate conflict.

- Learn the wonders of true compromise.

Life can feel overwhelming for a teen, so Chapter 12, "Building a Tool Belt," is dedicated to creating a Tool Belt for our teen. This begins with identifying the skills that teens need to incorporate into their lives to steer through the day-to-day challenges of growing up. It is important that our teen knows we are available as they master their independence. One way we can be helpful is by learning and sharing specific techniques that point them in the right direction. When we, as adults, have the right tools, it is easier to get any job done. Teens need access to their tools, too.

The Tool Box is a combination of what I have learned from my academic years, my private practice, seminars, conferences, workshops, books, children, parents, teachers, and other therapists. This collection of techniques is offered as a "menu" of ideas, and a list of tools as useful as the varied supply of nuts and bolts in the hardware store.

A young person's problems are just as diverse as the reason for a clogged drain or a leaky faucet. In either case, we try different tools until we find something that improves the situation. *The Tool Box* offers the best available ideas and tools, and all are practical and easy to use.

Remember: Find five tools of interest, try three, and discover the one that works!

CHAPTER 2

Opening the Toolbox

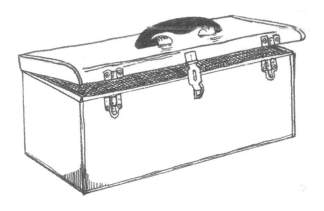

Basic Concepts

Many of us who live, work, or interact with teenagers have come to realize that there are times when we would like to try a new approach to these relationships. Some of us may recognize that we are repeating patterns and don't always like where they take us. We are now willing to alter the pattern or "change the dance."

If the porch steps are wobbling, we don't sell the house. We search through our variety of tools to fix the problem. Mechanics and carpenters need to learn about new and improved tools, and how to acquire the instruments that will allow them to better perform their jobs. We as parents need to update our tools as well so that we can help fix the problem at hand. We will have favorite tools that we use often, and we will use others less frequently. How do we know which tool to use and when?

Here are some basic concepts, which will make choosing the right tool less complicated.

The Job of a Parent

Parenting is hard work and is one of the longest jobs that we will do in our lives. There is no secret recipe; it is an ongoing effort of trial and error. The job description is always changing, the rewards are intangible, there is no retirement age, and the hours are unending.

It is very different to parent a teen in today's world than when our parents were raising us, although the main goal of our job description is the same: to keep our kids as healthy and safe as possible while we help them acquire the skills to become successful adults. The ways in which our parents accomplished this may not always be the best ways now. Times have changed. We might feel hypocritical, but it is okay to say, "Do what I say, not what I did."

The tools in this book will make the job of parenting easier.

The Job of a Teenager

It is a teenager's job to grow up and leave home. It is their goal for themselves and ultimately our goal for them. Teens need to figure out how to be independent and self-sufficient. They need to learn to navigate through a variety of tough situations. Part of this navigation is learning how to rely on themselves and make choices, and then to either suffer or enjoy the consequences.

Most significantly, it is their job to become their own person and figure out their occupation, style of dress, religion, politics, motivation, experimentation, and relationships.

The Teenage Brain

Groundbreaking research[1] has shown that the human brain transforms itself throughout the teen years. Current technology has enabled neuroscientists to view the inner workings of the living human brain. The collected evidence shows that extensive reorganizing occurs during adolescence; there is documented growth in the cerebral cortex and the parietal and frontal lobes. The frontal lobes help people weigh options, evaluate risks, consider consequences, and make good choices; it is also one of the *last areas of the brain to reach maturity.*

Once we understand that the connections between the *emotional centers* in the brain and the brain's *decision-making centers* are still developing in our 12- to 21-year-olds, we can begin to comprehend the unpredictability in our teen's decision-making process.

It is clear that the brain function of a teen is inconsistent at best. It is as if the teen is thinking with her feelings rather than her brain. The skill of using rational thinking to override intense feelings is not yet solid. Research[2] indicates that these skills are honed through physical changes and growth as well as through experiences and learning.

Consequently, a teenager can be a walking contradiction, at times looking and acting mature and responsible, and then moments later making foolish decisions that seem to come out of nowhere.

"What were you thinking?" we might ask. The answer truly seems to be that *they were not thinking.*

Again, the various components in the adolescent brain that are necessary to maneuver through the decision-making process have not yet solidified or fully matured. Analytical thinking—the skill of comprehending cause and effect, and the ability to foresee consequences of behavior and choice—has just begun to develop. Rational powers are not yet strong enough to be in charge all of the time.

In a calm, cool moment, a teen might very well "get" the right response to a situation; however, in a hot situation, such as when they are surrounded by peers, the emotional part of the brain overrules the more rational thought process. This is when stupid things tend to happen. Over time, the brain learns to balance itself.

The significant brain development that occurs during the teen years takes place in conjunction with life experience. Teens need this understanding and practice in order to establish the balance between thinking, feeling, and behaving. Teens are often exposed to situations where they think they are in control but lack reliable, rational thinking. We need to find ways to keep them safe as they cross the bridge between feeling like they know something and actually knowing it.

Our challenge is that we cannot easily assess where they are in this process of developing and maturing, yet we need them to stay healthy and safe while they explore and test.

The positive aspect of this inconsistency and turmoil is that the teen brain is certainly impressionable, and we as parents have the ability to affect its growth and direction. We have many opportunities to shift patterns, share, model behavior, discuss perspectives, lead by example, and reassure and support positive actions. *The Tool Box*, with its step-by-step approach, teaches parents how to be effective in identifying problem places, setting clear goals, and meeting objectives.

Change the Dance

Both the parent and the teen have their tasks, and so we do a little dance together: circling, joining hands, taking a bow or two, pulling apart, moving to the left ... Sometimes, though, we are bound to step on each other's feet.

This is the dance of all relationships. We are trying to do our parenting job while he is trying to do his job of becoming independent. There are many variations of this dance. If what we are doing is not working, then it is time to try something different. Being flexible and open to new ideas is the first step of the new dance.

Understand that, if we choose to do something differently, others will eventually have to respond to us in a new, altered way. If we have always waltzed, and we now choose to tango, our partner can no longer waltz with us. The footsteps have shifted and a new pattern of communication has begun.

This process can often feel quite awkward. Think of the confusion if one person attempts to waltz when the other has a tango in mind! During the transition, be prepared to trip over each other until the new rhythm settles in.

Emotional Literacy and Coping Skills

Communication is the most basic tool in our Tool Box. The basic skills of communication include the ability to express what we are feeling and thinking, and listen to and discern what another person is trying to express to us. Without these skills, it is impossible to communicate in a productive manner.

Our feelings influence everything we do. They affect our actions and our moods. They help determine how we think as well as the choices we make. Our feelings shift, vary, and change throughout the day. Sometimes they are very strong and can be overwhelming.

Often, we are faced with multiple emotions at the same time. When this happens, it is crucial to be able to identify our feelings, so we know how to name the thing with which we are dealing and stay in control.

Many teenagers are emotionally illiterate and unable to name their feelings. Sometimes they are quite competent in other ways, such as with sports, art, music, or school. Perhaps they are wonderful readers of books, but they may not know how to read their feelings nor do they know how to express what they are feeling.

Learning to read their feelings gives our teens a big head start in identifying and managing who they will be as adults because becoming emotionally literate is the beginning of becoming a successful adult. Mastering the building blocks of communication and identity, as well as the understanding and sharing of our emotions, are critical steps to growth and change.

Learning to handle everyday challenges successfully while balancing the significant issues of growing up safely and healthfully are the coping skills we aim to teach our teens.

Understanding Conflict and Compromise

What is conflict?

- Conflict is a natural part of everyday life.
- Conflict can be handled in positive or negative ways.
- Conflict can have either creative or destructive results.
- Conflict can be a positive force for personal growth and social change.

What is compromise?

- Compromise is not about giving in; it is about solving a problem.
- Compromise allows us to find solutions that are acceptable for everyone.
- Compromise can be a win/win scenario.

Conflict and compromise are part of all of our relationships and can show up in many different aspects of our lives. When people live, work, and play together, conflicts will happen. Most every dispute or conflict among people involves an attempt to meet a basic and important need for *belonging, power, freedom*, and *fun*. Our conflicts are important and need to be resolved in positive and creative ways.

Conflict, in and of itself, is not a bad thing. It is an opportunity to figure out who we are, who they are, and what our management styles are.

We deal with conflict all the time: in our families with children, spouses, parents, and siblings; with friends; at work with a boss or manager and fellow employees; with peers and neighbors in our community. Conflict can loosen up a stuck situation, allowing for movement and change.

Focus on Solutions

The tools in *The Tool Box* will give parents and teens the opportunity to try something new. We will spend very little effort blaming others or assigning fault because our focus will be on finding the solution.

Solutions are in front of us—not behind us.

Sometimes it is helpful to understand how things got off track but only if we use that information to move ahead.

By opening *The Tool Box,* we have made the decision to move out of the repetitive pattern of using the same methods to deal with the old patterns. Having new tools will help this process.

Understanding the root of a problem can give us the information we need to choose the correct tool and find the best solution. It is important to realize that, when we are looking for new solutions, we are focusing on future decisions and situations. The only thing we can hope to affect and change is the future.

The Mechanic

Parents: Rights and Responsibilities

Parenting is a hard job. It may be one of the most difficult, yet rewarding, challenges that we will encounter. We parent in the midst of everything else in our lives: work, aging parents, financial issues, and health concerns. There are many demands on our lives. Parents can feel confused, guilty, isolated, and exhausted. In our society, parenting is often unrecognized as the strenuous work that it is.

Adolescence is a time of change—not only for the teenager but for the parent as well. Parenting a teen takes focus, planning, experimentation, reflection, successes and failures, gut instincts, hunches, the ability to listen, limit setting, boundary stretching, love, instruction, patience, support, frustration, respect, flexibility, sharing ... the list is endless.

We want to "be there" for our kids to help them learn and gain control over their own lives. To do so, we need to understand their concerns, worries, and rationale for their choices, and listen to their point of view.

If we assume that the teen years are going to be a nightmare, it can be a self-fulfilling prophecy. Those who are expecting chaos and upheaval may be preparing themselves to overreact to small missteps. If we continually anticipate the worst from him, think what it does to his self-confidence!

While we are trying to be effective parents, we are struggling, too. We want to understand where our teens are "coming from," but that does not mean that we will accept or agree with their opinions, choices, and rationalizations. Ideally, working toward this understanding will enable us to communicate more effectively with our teens. If we comprehend their specific situation, we have a better chance of creating a response that is relevant and meaningful to our teen.

As parents, we can:

- *Slow things down.* Avoid being caught up in the immediacy of the moment or the demand of the teenager. Give the situation a chance to cool. It is okay to say, "I can't talk about this right now" or "Let's discuss this after dinner."

- *Listen first, talk second.* Learn to listen first. Before we respond with advice or comments, ask, "Is that everything you want to tell me?"

- *Feel hypocritical.* Just because *we* did "something" as a teen does not mean that we have to accept or support the same activity for our teen. We can give ourselves permission to make different choices.

- *Postpone a potentially difficult situation.* When we, or our teen, are tired, small issues can ignite enormous feelings. Know when not to engage in a potentially difficult conversation. Explain feelings of fatigue and the desire to wait.

- *Call other parents.* Confirming plans and checking on supervision are completely acceptable parental behaviors.

- *Cry.* Our teens can see us experiencing raw emotion. This may help them understand the complexity of emotions.

- *Separate our troubles from our teen's trouble.* Notice where our bad day ends and where our teen's bad day begins. If we are unable to keep our moods and issues separate, we may sabotage conversations.

- *Respect, support, and enjoy our kids.* Find the good in them. (Sometimes we may have to look very hard!) Show him respect and he will learn respect.

- *Spend one-on-one time.* Studies show that kids really care about what we think (even though they may never show it). Our attention reminds a teenager that she is important and that we like her company.

- *Use bribery as a tool.* Bribery works! It can be very useful to help teach consequences. A trade could be something like, "If you do X, then you have earned the right to do Y."

- *Ask for our teen's help.* Let her have an area of expertise. When we give her the opportunity to be good at something, it will feed her self-esteem and allow the relationship to grow.

- *Change our mind.* We do not have to fear being inconsistent occasionally. Sometimes this is a sign of our strength and not our weakness. Being able to take in new information and reevaluate a situation are signs of intelligence.

- *Be open to change.* Notice when the teen and the situation may have changed.

- *Learn new tricks and use improved tools.* It is okay to make a mistake, evaluate it, and then try something new.

ENDNOTES

1. David Dobbs, "Teenage Brains," *National Geographic* (October 2011).

2. *Ibid.*

PART II

Tools

CHAPTER 3

Nuts and Bolts

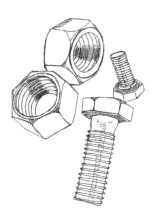

Get Connected by Listening and Communicating

We use nuts and bolts to make solid connections that help us keep them tight and, in the same way, good connections enable better communication.

The key to communication is listening, not talking.

When we listen, we are more likely to understand. This understanding helps us exchange ideas. The exchange of ideas enables us to brainstorm and problem solve. Misunderstandings happen because we don't listen to one another.

We often get distracted from listening when we are plotting how we will respond to what we think the other person is trying to say. It is very easy to get off track when we get ahead of a conversation.

Here are some nuts and bolts that keep us connected to our kids:

- Know how to listen.
- Use reflective listening.
- Ask clarifying questions.
- Learn phrases that help.
- Use communication to break frustrating cycles.
- Choose how to respond.

When we listen to a person, young or old, he feels understood, respected, and acknowledged. Listening is one of the first steps toward earning trust. Once there is trust, it feels safe to talk more honestly. Creating the listening tools, including asking questions and reflecting back what we hear, are the nuts and bolts in our Tool Box.

Mom is trying to get dinner on the table before she goes to a meeting. Fourteen-year-old Jim hollers from upstairs, "Mom! Get Kate out of my room! She's wrecking my stuff! I want a lock on my door. I *hate* her. You don't care about me!"

Mom has a choice of responses:

(A) Mom hollers up the stairs, "Just ignore her. She'll go away."

(B) Mom hollers up the stairs, "Kate, come downstairs. We'll get a cookie."

(C Mom goes upstairs and says, "Jim, please be patient. She's only five."

(D) Mom goes to Jim's room and says, "So, you're mad at Kate because she comes into your room without asking and always wants to play with your things, right?"

Several of these responses are tempting because we want to find a quick solution.

Going upstairs ourselves takes extra time and energy, which we don't always have. If we do go to the source of the disturbance, we would be more able to make a long-term change; however, by telling Jim to be patient, Mom would be adding to his growing frustration. Jim's patience is already gone, and asking him to ignore Kate doesn't show any understanding for how he feels. If Mom chooses to go upstairs and remove Kate, she has stopped the immediate problem but has done nothing to work on a long-term alternative.

Response (D) is an example of reflective listening and a clarifying question (described in the sections entitled "Use Reflective Listening" and "Ask Clarifying Questions" in this chapter).

In this option, Mom validates Jim's frustration with the situation. Mom is showing that she truly understands.

This method illustrates the beginning of finding a solution that might help. Once Jim feels that his mother understands how annoying it is to have his sister in his stuff, he will be calmer. Jim might even be able to figure out that his little sister is just trying to get his attention so he'll play with her. Perhaps Jim will decide, on his own, to put his things away so Kate won't have such easy access, or that the simple action of closing his door might dissuade Kate from coming in.

Whatever the solution, it is hard for Jim or Mom to find it in anger. Both Mom and Jim need to connect. This connection, like nuts and bolts, brings together separate parts so they can work together.

Yelling up and down the stairs is not a good connection. In Option (D), Mom goes to the scene of the problem. Her presence assures Jim that she is ready to listen. After she listens, they may be able to get closer to a solution. She listens first, and then talks. She uses the listening "bolt" and then the "nut" to connect to Jim.

Know How to Listen

Here are three basic things to do when trying to listen to our teen:

(1) *Give our full attention.* We need to stop what we are doing—whether it's sweeping the floor, washing the dishes, or reading the newspaper. Make eye contact.

(2) *Watch his body language.* Is he tense, anxious, or teary eyed?

(3) *Be a part of the conversation by actively listening.* We can rephrase what he has said and repeat it back to him, so we both know that it is right. He hears that we care.

Creating a connection with our teen is a bit like being a baseball outfielder. We might not see much action but, when that ball comes our way, we must be ready! Making ourselves available is crucial since we don't always know when they will need us. If we are paying attention, our children will learn that they can rely on us.

When we are listening, it is not the time to put a spin on an issue or situation, or make it a life lesson. It is the time to:

- Let the teenager talk it through, ask questions, and contemplate different answers.

- Allow them to validate the wide—and often contradicting—range of emotions, and perhaps empathize with a similar example from our own lives. This will help our teen learn how to process a situation.

"Processing" is when we take the time to think through a situation. It is a chance to study actions and reactions, identify emotions and feelings, look for natural consequences, and brainstorm ways to move forward.

Tone of voice, body language, and attention are important ingredients in how we listen. Sarcasm, teasing, and yelling are not helpful. We are trying to get our teen engaged in a conversation. We need to offer our full attention without distraction. We can touch our teen on the shoulder, give him a hug, and show him that we are ready to listen.

It is best not to jump in with our own solution. Keep listening, asking questions, and listening more. He will eventually come up with some answers of his own.

Jim: I hate her messing with my things.

Mom: How did she get in here?

Jim: I left the door open.

Mom: Oh, the door was open and she walked in?

Jim: Yeah, but from now on I am going to keep it closed forever.

Mom: Do you think that will help?

Jim: You won't let me put a lock on the door, so all I can do is put my stuff away before I go out. Then, if she comes in, maybe she can't get hold of my stuff so easily.

Mom: Jim, that's a great idea. Good thinking! Let's see how that works.

Use Reflective Listening

The nuts and bolts of listening use a technique called "reflective listening." Listen to the whole story. Let the teen get it all out, even if she is only venting. Do not interrupt. Do not try to reason with her or offer a defense.

Sometimes it helps to take notes. We can jot her comments down on a pad of paper and make notes of thoughts we want to revisit. If she makes untrue statements, such as "You hate my boyfriend," "You don't trust me," and "There is no way you could ever understand," continue to listen.

Let her tell her story. It is her story, her emotions, and her understanding of the situation. By listening, we might be able to better comprehend where she is coming from and see her reality.

Avoid name calling, threatening, judging, or criticizing. Be aware that our tone of voice and body language affect our verbal message. Most of us cannot stand it when our kids sigh, roll their eyes, mimic, or gesture at us. We need to model respect by not displaying any of these responses to them.

This kind of listening is not easy.

There will come a time when we can review what she has said, introduce our version of the situation, and share our reaction.

It requires that we try to listen without concentrating on what to say next. *It means that we listen without giving advice.* Make the effort to understand her point of view and respect that it is her opinion. By doing this, we are not necessarily agreeing with her but are instead allowing her the right to her opinion.

Ask Clarifying Questions

After hearing her whole story, it is best to respond with questions. Questions are the way a good listener will try to understand completely what the teen is saying, what she wants, and how she feels.

We can use questions that summarize or reflect back what we think she is trying to express. These questions usually start with something like, "Do you mean …?" or "I think what you are saying is …"

Ask questions, but do not turn the event into an inquisition. The point of asking questions is to understand the situation and help the teen communicate. Keep the questions open ended by limiting questions that can be answered with yes or no.

Avoid the "How do you feel?" question. Get her talking by asking action-oriented questions. Starting with too many "feeling questions" can send her packing! Stay away from the "whys." (Most of us don't have a clue as to why we do what we do!)

The goal of asking questions is to generate information and help her open up. The following questions will help to get her talking about the details of the story:

- "What happened?"
- "Who was there?"
- "What did they say?"
- "Where were you?"
- "What did you do then?"
- "Then what happened?"
- "Is there anything else?"

Once the teenager has stated the "facts" and explained the scenario, we can begin to ask clarifying questions. These questions show that we have been listening and have a basic familiarity with the series of events. We need to confirm with her that we have a proper understanding of her whole story. It is crucial that we get the complete story *so we know that we are responding to the main issue.*

For example, if our teen is upset about her boyfriend because he has been talking about sex all the time, we may react with the "You are too young to be having sex!" talk. However, if we let her get her story out completely, we might learn that she is feeling ambivalent about having sex and is very uncomfortable in the relationship. She may actually be looking for advice on how to back away from the relationship.

Here are some suggestions:
- "So what you are telling me is …"
- "Can you give me an example?"
- "Tell me more."

- "That sounds hard."
- "Are you saying that...?"
- "Why is that important?"
- "I'm not sure I understand. Can you explain it to me?"
- "Let me make sure that I get what you are saying."
- "How important is this to you?"
- "What do you want to happen?"
- "What are you thinking of doing about this?"
- "What can I do to help?"
- "Are you mad or upset with me?"
- "Has anything like this happened before? If it has, how did you handle it? What would you have done differently? What would you do next time?"
- "How are you feeling now?"
- "I still don't understand. Can you try explaining it a different way?"

Validate her feelings. Make observations and give her a chance to confirm or explain things again. Remember: *We can understand her point of view without agreeing with her.* It will show her that we care about her and the way she feels.

Our goal is to be as direct and honest as we can. Teens are often smarter than we first realize. Whenever possible, we need to continue with these questions until we have found out her real issue. Then, we can help put the base issue on the table.

Learn Phrases That Help

Here are examples of statements that can help when navigating a new path of communication:

- "No wonder you feel so angry / sad / hurt / anxious / tense / stressed / left out."
- "Now that I understand how you see it, I get why you are so upset."
- "It's hard when everything feels so overwhelming and out of control."

- "I am glad that you told me. It is important to me that you can share things like this with me."

- "I really like it when you ..."

- "I am annoyed / angry / disappointed that you did this, but I will always love you."

- "What do you think I am trying to say?"

- "I wish I did have all of the answers, but I don't."

When someone feels truly heard, it can have a calming effect. *We need to be calm and stable before we can move to the next step: figuring what to do with the current situation.*

It helps to recognize that there are at least two ways of seeing a situation and that most viewpoints have some merit. Our teen may see the situation one way and we may see it another. He will see that our view has some merit if we are able to see that his view has value, too.

This drawing[1] is a great example. Some people see an old witchy woman; some see a beautiful young girl. They are both in this picture. Both views are accurate even though they are very different.

Sometimes we have to relax and try to see or understand what someone else does. Most likely, we already have patterns that push each other's buttons. We may need to retrain ourselves in how we respond to our teen.

Mom is annoyed that Cindy is complaining about school again. Mom has had this conversation with Cindy 20 times already. Neither of them is actually listening to the other, so they both repeat themselves and have the same reactions. Mom and Cindy are frustrated that they cannot make any progress and feel stuck in a pattern.

They need to change the dance.

Cindy: They gave us so much stupid homework!

Mom: You say that every night. If you spent less time complaining and just got busy on it, it would be over sooner.

What happens when this type of conversation takes place every day? As the above response illustrates, we have a habitual reaction to our teen's behavior. Now that we have realized it, perhaps we can stop ourselves from the knee-jerk reaction of a parent who is tired from all of the complaining.

When we feel ourselves get that panicky feeling of "here we go again" or the sense that things are going to "heat up and fall apart," we can try to step back for a moment or two and take a little breather.

In the below response, we show an example where Mom reflects back to Cindy what she is saying. This will let Cindy know that Mom is hearing her.

Mom: What else is going on besides all that homework?

Cindy: School *stinks*! My English teacher hates me and tries to ruin my life. I think she loves to embarrass me. The principal *always* agrees with her, no matter what I say. They never listen. I *hate* Spanish 2. It is like Spanish 5! I just can't *do* it anymore. I want to see Pete. He is the only person in the world who cares about me.

Mom: So what you are saying is that you are angry because your English teacher is mean and unfair, the principal automatically sides with your teacher without even knowing the whole story, and Spanish 2 is harder than you expected. You need a break from school. You really need to see your boyfriend, and you don't think I understand how you are feeling.

This response will help Cindy articulate what she is feeling and realize that Mom is paying attention. *It might also enable her to recognize that the different things stressing her out are truly separate items, which she can handle individually.* This recognition can then make the situation feel less overwhelming.

By reflecting to Cindy, Mom is validating her feelings—not agreeing or disagreeing with Cindy. This is the beginning of identifying the problem and figuring out how to address the issues.

The goal is to avoid letting the situation become a fight between Cindy and Mom because the issues are not between the two of them. If Mom can focus and shift the conversation to the things that she can help Cindy change, their conversation will be more productive.

Use Communication to Break Frustrating Cycles

We may cloud communication with anger, silence, apathy, or resentment. It is important to note that *blaming is not helpful.* Each of us is responsible for our own behavior. Using communication to break the negative patterns of responding is the first step.

Reflective listening is much more than repeating our teen's words back to her. It is a cooperative effort to figure out what is going on with our teen and show her that we are trying to understand what she is feeling. Once she feels understood, she is more likely to be open to hearing what we are trying to say.

Eye contact, body language, and touch are important. *Avoid nagging, teasing, and lecturing.* No one likes this sort of treatment. Our message will get lost.

We don't get what we don't ask for. For example, if we want our teen to do—or not do—something, we need to express this desire. Take the time to figure out what is important to you. We need to take the responsibility to say what we need.

For example, we may say, "I know that I may have never told you this before, but it is important to me that …

- … you do well in school because I never graduated."
- … you look presentable in church because it's important to the family."
- … you not overeat because I was a fat kid."

We may also say, "I realize that it is partly my fault because I have never shared this with you before, but I am hoping that maybe we can work on this."

Developing communication skills takes practice. Rehearse little things that are not a big deal or emotionally loaded. Learning new ways of communicating is not easy, but the only way to improve and change old habits is to practice.

Being specific with a comment or request is an easy place to start. A vague request like "Please clean up the living room" might not get the desired results; however, here are some examples of useful statements:

- "Please put the newspaper into the recycling bin."
- "Bring the dishes from the table and put them into the kitchen sink."

- "Please load the dishwasher."
- "I am exhausted tonight. Would you please read a bedtime story to your little brother?"

We may find that our opinion on a given topic is often not enough to convince our teen to agree with our point of view. Eventually, her own experience will bring home a new understanding. If we can help her process her choices, actions, and reactions, she will find her own teaching moments.

Ultimately, this is our goal. We want our teens to mature into independent adults who know how to handle themselves in many situations and who will be able to reason within themselves to find good solutions. If we overprotect them, how will they be able to sharpen their own problem-solving skills?

Choose How to Respond

If we train ourselves to think before we respond, we will succeed in changing the patterns in our relationships. A key factor to remember is that *we can choose how we communicate and respond.* Sometimes we need to listen for the feelings that are behind the spoken words.

Sarah, upset about the seventh-grade play, comes home whining.

"I didn't get a part in the play. *Everybody* was better than me. All my friends got all of the good parts."

Mom: Sarah, you sound like a brat! Why must you whine about *everything*? You had a big part in the play last year. You know that you can't *always* get a part. Besides, you are having such a hard time with math right now, and you could use that extra time to put more effort into pre-algebra.

Sarah: I *knew* you wouldn't understand. You *never* do!

Here's an alternative response:

Mom: Sounds like you feel left out and that you really wanted to be a part of the play.

Sarah: Yeah, I feel like such a *loser*. What am I going to do for the next two months while they are all having fun in rehearsals?

Mom: It will be hard not to be part of something that most of your friends are doing.

Sarah: They will have all of this stuff to talk about and I won't know any of it. They probably already have jokes that I don't get.

Mom: Hmm, that is really tough. Maybe you could volunteer to be on the stage crew. Then you could be involved in a different way.

Sarah: That would be better than nothing. I'll talk to the director tomorrow.

Sometimes we need to shift gears mid-conversation. For example, Tom's soccer team just lost a big game. Tom was the goalie and he did not play well.

Dad: What the heck were you *thinking* out there?

Tom: Thanks, Dad. That really helps. Do you want to say anything *else* to make me feel bad?

Dad: Well, if you'd just concentrate more, you could have pulled this off today.

Tom: You think I wasn't trying? You think I don't care? I *hate* this stupid game!

Here's how Dad can reverse the confrontation:

Dad: Hey, I am sorry. I did not mean to hurt your feelings.

Tom: Sure … whatever!

Dad: It is tough enough to lose without someone adding to the frustration. I know that being a goalie is hard. Sometimes, like today, the whole game sits on your shoulders.

Tom: No kidding. I wish you could help me instead of criticize me.

Dad: Well, the last few times you said you didn't want my help.

Tom: But I need to try some stuff on my own!

Dad: Okay, let's try this. I won't try to help you unless you ask for it. That way, you won't feel like I am nagging and I won't feel like you don't care about my help.

Tom: Okay, that sounds good.

Dad has done a couple of things in the above dialogue:

- He has validated how Tom feels and shown some real understanding. His empathy helped Tom calm down.

- He was able to outline a path for going forward that they could both accept.

Susan, a sophomore, moans at dinner, "Mr. Loner is such a *loser*. He picks on me all of the time. It is not fair. I am *never* going to pass his class!"

Dad: Life is not always fair, you know. Sometimes we have tough teachers. I doubt he is really picking on you. He's probably tough on everybody. He can't flunk you if you work hard.

Susan: Um, yeah, he can … he is such a jerk! I don't want to take his dumb class anyway. I *hate* school!

Dad: Don't be ridiculous, Susan. You can't hate school because of one history class.

Susan: You've no idea, Dad. Forget I mentioned it. You're on his side. You *always* are!

Here's an alternative response:

Dad: You seem frustrated and mad. It really stinks to feel picked on.

Susan: He always tries to make me seem stupid.

Dad: What is it that you are studying in class right now?

Susan: The Civil War. It is so boring. Everything is about dates.

Dad: Yeah, I remember having to memorize all of those battle sites and generals' names. It seemed irrelevant to me at the time, too.

Susan: You studied U.S. history?

Dad: Yes, it has been a requirement for a long time. Hey, let me see your textbook. Maybe I can help. You know there are some interesting stories …

All of the above alternative response examples show a way to engage in a conversation that does not put the teen on the defensive. It encourages them to experience upset feelings and look at the bigger situation.

The parent is helping the teen learn to address the problem by providing descriptive words, which help identify what is going on and connect it to an event that occurred. All of the parents found a way to do this in their life.

By filling in the blanks in the below formula, we can help our teen begin to untangle the emotional situation:

"You seem both _____ and _____ because_____."

Here's another way to break the cycle:

Dad is frustrated that Billy has not yet done his chores. He hates that it is almost noon and the day is wasting away. He wishes that Billy would be more motivated to get things done.

Dad: Have you done your chores yet? It is almost noon!

Billy: No. Would you quit nagging me? I'll do them later!

Here's an alternative response where Dad is trying to put a positive spin on the question, emphasizing that there is something else he'd like to do with Billy.

Dad: Hey, Billy, if you do your chores by 2 o'clock, we can go hit some balls at the batting cages. Baseball tryouts are coming up and it'd be fun to get outside.

Billy: That'd be cool, Dad. I can be done in about a half an hour.

We called this chapter "Nuts and Bolts" because *communication skills hold relationships together.* Listening is the tool that keeps us connected to other people. Learning to communicate positively is important. Often, in stressful times, we do not communicate well. Under stress, we might hear a lot of noise inside our heads and cannot hear others.

If we want to communicate well, make changes, and improve relationships, the best way to do this is by listening well and communicating thoughtfully. Demanding, nagging, or ordering our teen to change will not help.

We need to practice keeping an open mind with our teen. Listen to what they are saying. Listen to their fears and concerns as well as their hopes and dreams.

When we have information that we want to give our teen, we especially need to remember that ultimately people listen best when they feel heard. The better informed our teens are, the more apt they are to act responsibly. When we see a misstep, we are able to determine what they still need to know.

This is our best road map for understanding where our teens are coming from and where they want (or need) to go. If we can get in sync with their thinking, then we have a better chance of influencing their direction and their plans for getting there.

We have many opportunities to influence our teens, and most require good communication.

ENDNOTE

1. For a history of this figure see http://mathworld.wolfram.com/YoungGirl-OldWomanIllusion.html.

CHAPTER 4

The Level

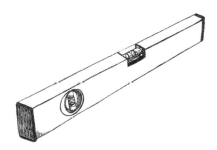

Stability: Encouraging Emotional Literacy

A "level" is a tool with a bubble in it. When we hold up a level against the wall when hanging a picture, the bubble lines up in the center of the marker, and we know that things are straight.

We want to know the same kind of thing when it comes to our kids. We do not want to guess what they are feeling. For example, sometimes our teen looks like she's really mad at us but, in actual fact, she may be angry, scared, or annoyed with someone else. We want to know what is really going on.

Many teens do not know how to express what they are feeling. They do not have the skills to handle everyday challenges successfully, especially the more significant issues of growing up safely and healthfully. When teens feel truly unprepared for these situations, their feelings of self-doubt and insecurity can be crippling.

It is helpful to consider that our culture is changing fast: socially, emotionally, economically, and technologically. The ramifications of this cultural trend are far reaching and often confusing. We cannot avoid change. We need to adapt our coping skills to meet these changes and challenges, and identifying and understanding our feelings are part of the challenge.

I have found that many of my adolescent clients are emotionally illiterate. A simple question, such as "You seem upset. What's wrong?" often gets a response such as "I don't know." Many times, they really *don't* know, and this can be as frustrating to them as it is to us.

- Did they skip lunch?
- Are they overtired?
- Did someone hurt their feelings?
- Did they not do well on a test?
- Are they truly overwhelmed?

The possibilities are endless.

Teens need emotional literacy tools to help them identify and express what they are feeling. These tools are like levels, helping to keep them straight and balanced, which gives them the ability to focus on the current task.

HALT

Understanding what we are feeling is complicated. Using the acronym HALT, which means **H**ungry / **A**ngry / **L**onely / **T**ired, is an easy place to start. It is a technique that we can practice ourselves, teach our teen, and model for each other. Once we can begin to identify the feeling, we can more easily figure out what we need to do in order to feel better.

Hungry

When we get that crazy, worked-up feeling, we can remind ourselves to stop—or HALT. For example, we can ask ourselves, "Am I hungry? Did I work through lunch? Did I skip my afternoon snack?"

If the answer is "yes," then we can help ourselves by realizing that we need to eat something. Knowing this before we enter the home zone can give us the key to navigating our reentry.

Instead of losing our temper with the kids because the dog is barking, backpacks are piled on the floor, or they are bombarding us with their latest squabble, we can realize that we need a few minutes to get some cheese and crackers in our belly.

Sharing this epiphany with our kids will enlighten them to the fact that we need a few minutes to recoup. We are showing them that it is important to identify our needs and take care of ourselves first so we will be better able to take care of theirs.

Angry

Perhaps it is not hunger. Maybe we are feeling angry. If we take a moment to reflect on our day, we may recognize that we are upset because we lost an account at work or a client was unhappy with something; maybe we got a speeding ticket on the way home.

Being able to discern that what we are feeling is anger, and then being able to clarify what we are angry about, will help us before we unknowingly project that anger onto someone else. When the kids greet us at the door with their problems, dilemmas, requests, needs, and desires, we can say, "Hey, guys. I had a tough day at work. Can you give me a few minutes?" This is best accomplished when we take a moment and scan our day. Eventually, the kids will appreciate the heads up and understand that we need a little space.

Lonely

Maybe we are not feeling hungry or angry, but we are experiencing a feeling of loneliness. Perhaps we are feeling sad about something. Being able to identify the feeling is the beginning of the road map to figuring out what we need to do to feel better.

If we are feeling lonely, we should not go home and eat! We can pick up the phone and call a friend, ask one of the kids for a hug, and find other ways to connect with people.

Tired

If the overwhelming feeling is exhaustion, then we should respect it. This is not a time to be social and project our feelings onto others. We can accept that tired feeling and keep our plate clear until we have had a chance to recoup our energy.

Using HALT for Teenagers

The four questions in the HALT acronym work just as well for teenagers. Perhaps she skipped lunch, one of her teachers gave her a hard time about a school assignment, she is feeling excluded by the gang, or she stayed up too late last night.

The simplicity of using HALT encourages her to slow down and actually think about what she is feeling and not react in an emotional moment. *It teaches that we do different things for different issues.* Once we can identify what we are feeling, we can begin to ask for what we truly need. This lets her (and us) feel more in control and prepared.

Beth comes home from the school dance. She storms into the family room and rants about her sister Lisa, who has moved her stuff and is a complete jerk. Why didn't someone think to remind her that tomorrow is Grandma's birthday party?

Mom: Do not walk into this room and start yelling at people! We are just sitting here watching a movie and relaxing. It is rude of you to barge in and interrupt without any regard to what is going on here. Please leave and reenter the room like a human being!

Beth: Fine. No one cares about me anyway.

Here's an alternative response:

Mom: Hey, slow down a second. You sound pretty torqued. Let's go into the kitchen. What is going on?

Beth: I just *told* you. Weren't you listening?

Mom: I heard what you said, but you came into the house angry. I understand that you are mad that your stuff got moved, but let's stop and figure it out. I know it may sound silly, but let's do the HALT thing. Are you hungry? Did you have any dinner before you left for the dance? Did something happen at the dance that made you angry? Did you hang out with your friends at the dance? Who was there? You know you stayed up really late last night, working on the history project, and you had a hard time waking up this morning. Maybe you are more tired than you thought.

As Mom walks through the HALT questions with Beth, they can begin to decipher the larger picture. Yes, Beth may be upset with her sister, and annoyed about her things being moved, but it is important for Beth to see how things have built up through the course of the day. If she can begin to identify where she was vulnerable, Beth can realize what she needs to do to feel better.

While the HALT process helps to identify basic, simplified feelings and needs, we should continue to explore the wider array of emotions with our teens. Being able to more clearly express feelings and emotions helps to create a broader picture and understand a situation better.

Words for Feelings

Below are examples of a wide array of emotions. Even within the same spectrum of emotion, we show an extensive assortment of feelings, each of which has a slightly different need requiring attention.

Words Describing a Variety of Positive Emotions and Feelings

Think of the difference between "fabulous" and "content" or "peaceful" and "giddy.

affectionate	ecstatic	hopeful	relieved
bemused	elated	interested	satisfied
blissful	enthusiastic	joyous	silly
charmed	excited	jubilant	smart
cheerful	fabulous	loving	smug
confident	fortunate	marvelous	soothed
content	giddy	optimistic	thrilled
curious	glad	peaceful	tickled
delighted	gratified	pleased	turned on
determined	high	proud	wonderful
dreamy			

Words Describing a Variety of Hurt Feelings

How different are the needs behind "neglected" and "cheated" or "jilted" and "abused"?

abused	deserted	helpless	pained
awful	devalued	humiliated	persecuted
betrayed	diminished	ignored	put down
cheated	disappointed	insulted	regretful
confused	discouraged	intimidated	rotten
crippled	dreadful	isolated	slighted
damaged	embarrassed	jilted	snubbed
defeated	envious	neglected	terrible
deflated	forgotten	oppressed	upset
deprived			

Words Describing a Variety of Negative Feelings

Feeling "lonely" is different than feeling "offended," and feeling "disgusted" is different than being "scared."

afraid	dismayed	inept	revolted
aggravated	embarrassed	infuriated	riled
aggressive	enraged	irritated	sad
alienated	exasperated	jealous	scared
annoyed	exhausted	lonely	shocked
anxious	fearful	mad	sorry
apathetic	frightened	mediocre	steamed
appalled	frustrated	miserable	stressed
ashamed	furious	nauseated	suspicious
bashful	guilty	offended	ticked off
bitter	helpless	outraged	troubled
bored	hostile	overwhelmed	unworthy
cautious	horrified	paranoid	upset
cranky	inadequate	powerless	useless
depressed	incapable	provoked	vicious
disappointed	incensed	repulsed	wary
disgusted	incompetent	resentful	worried

"How Do You Feel Today?"

Sometimes it helps to have a visual version of this chart:

How dissimilar is "peaceful" from "thrilled"?

"Worried" from "repulsed"?

"Deprived" from "damaged"?

"Helpless" from "mediocre" or "inferior"?

How might our reaction differ to our teen if he were able to say that he felt "aggravated" or "inadequate"?

Our language provides us with a huge vocabulary to be able to identify specific nuances of feelings. If our teen can find the right word to tell us how he feels, then we have a clue as to where to begin to help. The words become our road map.

Perhaps we can find a time to share these lists with our teen. It is similar to when we graduate our young children from a simple box of eight colored crayons to the larger array of 24, and then eventually the assortment of 164 shades of color. When their pictures require more details and hues, we offer them the bigger box.

We need to use these words and expose our children and teens to the nuances of meaning. As with crayons, when the time is appropriate, we can introduce new words. We may find the opportunity to compare and contrast a few words, and really talk about which ones best describe a certain feeling.

Think Globally Versus Locally

Another helpful skill is to ask ourselves, "Is this problem global or local?" Global issues are those problems upon which we do not have a direct impact, such as things that are truly beyond our control; however, we can affect local issues. It can be very helpful to categorize issues this way to figure out how to respond and which tool to use.

Our teen is fuming because bad weather cancelled his baseball game. That is a global concern for us because we can't change the weather. If he doesn't have a ride to the game—a local issue—we may be able to help him find one.

It is important to let him feel frustration, anger, or embarrassment. It is good to listen to him as he expresses his feelings. His emotions are real. *The feelings may not be rational, but they are real emotions.* Later in the conversation, there will be time to point out the fact that there are situations through which we all have to work, and that we all have had bad teachers and difficult bosses. The first step is to listen and help him identify his overriding feelings and emotions.

Litmus paper is a thin paper film used in chemistry class to test the acid and alkaline levels of a substance, and I have used this metaphor with teens. Instead of testing for acidity, we are testing for global versus local issues. This is another way of figuring out how to respond to a situation.

It is very helpful to ascertain the type of problem or situation with which we are dealing. As I mentioned above, we cannot control the weather, but we can remember to bring an umbrella, which is an appropriate response to a global issue.

Clarity

One of the reasons that communication fails is that we are unable to say what we mean. The clearer we are in our own head, the better we can communicate with others.

Slamming the door, 16-year-old Linda storms into the house and says, "I *hate* my life. I never want to see Susie again!" Agitated and angry, she begins to sob.

Dad: How many times have I told you not to slam the door! There is always so much drama in your life. It is almost funny.

Linda: You are so mean! You don't care about me. You never even try to understand me!

Here's another way to respond:

Dad: You sound pretty angry. Come tell me what happened.

Linda: Everyone thinks I am a total geek. I can't show may face in school on Monday. Susie was supposed to meet me at the party, but she never came! I *hate* her. I was the only one there by myself!

Dad: You must have been very embarrassed because she didn't show up. I know it doesn't feel good to be alone in a situation like that. Have you called Susie to find out why she didn't come to the party?

Linda: It was so bad. Everyone just stared at me like I was an idiot. No one talked to me all night. I got so mad!

Dad: Why don't you give Susie a call and make sure that she is okay. Maybe she couldn't get a ride or maybe she got sick. Didn't you mention that she had a fight with her mother? Maybe she was grounded.

Linda: I forgot about that. I'll call her now.

We can try to imagine how our teen feels and help her find the right words to describe her feelings. When we can find a way to validate what our teen is feeling, she will begin to feel less alone. As she calms down, she will be more open to recognizing the bigger picture.

In the second response, Dad is helping Linda identify the emotion behind her statement of anger. Getting Linda to slow down and think—instead of react—is a good first step. Dad is giving Linda a suggestion so she can gather more information and find out what happened to Susie.

This technique enables Linda to feel more in control. She does not like the feeling of "losing it." Linda needs to be reminded that she can handle this emotional place. She is now prepared to deal with the situation. *Instead of feeling victimized and out of control, her self-esteem is reestablished and she can move forward.*

Finding clarity empowers us, and our teens, to have more control and be better prepared for the challenges that come our way. If our teen does not have clarity, she will trip over herself (and others) as she tries to navigate the situation. When Linda feels "ready" and in control, she will feel better about herself.

Heather comes home and sinks into the sofa, picks up the TV remote, and declares, "I'm bored!"

Mom: How could you *possibly* be bored? You have just spent the entire afternoon with your friends hanging out at the mall. I let you do exactly what you wanted, and you come home and complain! I just don't know how to make you happy!

Here's another response that Mom could have used:

Mom: Bored of what?

Heather: Everything!

Mom: I thought you were at the mall with Stacy and Liz?

Heather: I was. They got annoying.

Mom: Sounds like you weren't having a good time with them.

Heather: How could I? They just giggle and whisper to each other.

Mom: It's no fun to be left out.

Heather: No kidding.

Mom: So they didn't include you in their secrets and you got bored watching them have a good time?

Heather: Yeah, it really hurt my feelings that they could be so bratty.

Mom: You sound kind of sad and lonely.

Heather: Well, that's part of it. It was also embarrassing to be with them but not to be in on the joke.

Mom: So it sounds like you weren't bored but perhaps frustrated that you were being left out.

Heather: Yeah, I feel really sad.

Mom: I am sorry that you feel sad. I know that you were looking forward to hanging out with Stacy and Liz. You must be very disappointed.

Heather: When I left the mall, I felt like crying.

In the second response, Mom is trying to help Heather separate all of the issues that are stressing her out. Heather cannot affect some of the concerns; others are in her direct power and would benefit from prompt attention. This process takes patience on our part as we help our teen become more aware of what is influencing her and how to navigate through the situation.

Having the ability to identify stressors (e.g., the social pieces of feeling left out, embarrassed, sad, and hurt) is like "taming the beast." It is much easier to create an action plan when we have a good grip on the priorities.

When we ask questions, avoid confrontation, and uncover underlying issues, these three steps will help deescalate the situation. Heather begins to relax because Mom actually seems to understand how she is feeling. In this place of understanding, Mom and Heather can have a conversation of value and significance.

Taking the time to untangle and digest our own wide range of emotions is a coping skill that we all need. We become more effective when we can accurately express ourselves. If anger is masking our feelings of loneliness or fatigue, how can we get our true needs met?

We need to help our teens discover this wonderful "trick" of figuring out what they are actually feeling so they can feel better about themselves and their situations. Our society will continue to change and shift around us. Our ability to read ourselves accurately will enable us to navigate whatever challenges life throws in our direction.

CHAPTER 5

The Wrench

Conflict: The Torque Matters

We use a wrench to get the right amount of tension by adjusting how tight or loose something needs to be. This is valuable information when discussing conflict.

- Conflict is a natural part of everyday life.

- Conflict can be handled in positive or negative ways.

- Conflict can have either creative or destructive results.

- Conflict can be a positive force for personal growth and social change.

Many people fear conflict. They perceive it as a negative experience and try to avoid it completely. Ironically, conflict is an important component of all of our relationships and is unavoidable. Learning how to deal with differences is a necessary life skill for everyone.

Who really likes doors slamming and kids sulking? These signs of conflict can make us feel queasy. Parents wonder what they did wrong when their child clams up or makes a snide remark. Sometimes, we have done nothing seriously wrong but are simply facing a child's growth spurt. If this is the case, we need to use a different tool to manage the situation.

It is a brave and constructive challenge to view the signs of conflict as an opportunity for change and growth. It is a chance to get unstuck and change the patterns in a relationship. If we can look at a situation and begin to recognize that conflict happens for a variety of reasons, we are more apt to find a workable solution.

For example, conflict can occur when there are miscommunications, misunderstandings, misinformation, or insufficient resources. Conflict also occurs because of our basic needs for love, connection, independence, safety, understanding, fun, creativity, meaningfulness, and a sense of accomplishment.

The reasons behind a conflict are wide and varied. It is important to discover the issue creating the conflict in order to figure out the proper tools to use in our approach to find resolution.

Different problems use different solutions. It is important to identify an objective. For example:

- Is our goal to reduce the number of times our child slams the door or minimize the time she spends sulking in her room?

- Do we hope to learn what is causing her to withdraw from the family?

If there is a common end goal for parents and the teen, we can focus on working together to solve the problem. In other words, if we know where we are going, then we are far more likely to get there faster if we work *with* our teen. This chapter will show some tools of engagement, which we can use to tighten and loosen situations, like a wrench.

Sixteen-year-old Julie is making plans for the weekend. She is planning to go to the Friday night football game with a few friends and hang out afterwards. Julie would like to have her curfew extended to 11:30 p.m. because they might go bowling, out for Chinese food, or maybe to Stan's house.

Julie's friend Lisa has her dad's car, so Mom doesn't need to worry about driving her anywhere, and Lisa can even bring Julie home afterwards. Julie is very proud of her good planning and the fact that she doesn't need to bug Mom for a ride.

Julie's mom is having all of her buttons pushed: Her daughter will be hanging out, with no specific plans, and driving around in a carload of teenagers with an extended curfew. Mom feels that Julie is being sneaky and trying to hide her plans. Mom and Julie are headed down a well-worn path of misunderstanding.

Mom: I'm not sure that I like the sound of all this.

Julie (interrupting): You never let me do *anything*!

Mom: I hate fighting with you about everything. How many times have I told you that I don't like you driving around in a car with a load of kids? How many times have I told you that I don't like it when you have vague plans? I never know where you are!

Julie: Oh, you'd just like me to stay home all of the time and never do anything.

Mom: That's it ... you are grounded!

The yelling begins. Unfortunately, we often feel that, when someone isn't doing what we want them to do, they are not listening. We get louder and hope that they will pay more attention. In actuality, the basic needs of independence and safety are at play here.

We also need to be aware of going into new situations and *expecting the same negative outcome.* When we are looking for the negative, we close ourselves off to the possibility of a different (and perhaps positive) result. Often, we end up getting exactly what we did *not* want but certainly what we *expected.*

Mom and Julie have already anticipated the other's response. Mom is sure that Julie is up to something and that she is losing control of her daughter. Julie is sure that Mom does not understand and is refusing to let her grow up.

The best way to encourage new behavior is to stay positive. Phrases such as "Didn't I just tell you?," "I have asked you 10 times," and "How many times have I told you?" imply a certain amount of "Here we go again!"

Here's an alternative response:

Mom: Sounds like a night with a lot of options! I can tell that you have been working on these plans.

Julie: It is a pain in the butt to get everyone to agree on a plan. I am psyched that Lisa can get her dad's car because then I don't have to bug you for rides all over the place.

Mom: I appreciate that you are not asking me to drive you everywhere. When do you think you might be able to narrow down the plans a bit? I get uncomfortable if I don't know where you are.

Julie: Well, I guess we'll decide when everyone is together at the game.

Mom: I know that I may sound like an overprotective mom, but do you think you could call me from the game and let me know what the plans are? Once we know what you're going to do, then we can come up with a reasonable time for you to come home after going bowling or out for food.

Instead of expecting the worst from Julie, Mom acknowledges her efforts and opens the door for real communication. We need to be aware that our fears for our children as well as our expectations of others can distort our ability to see what is really going on.

Often, we project onto others what we expect based on our own experiences. We interpret our teen's behavior without taking the time to listen to what they are trying to say. We assume that we know what they are thinking and feeling and their intentions for behaving a certain way; however, we may be off base.

Mom has used the imaginary wrench—a tool that makes a tighter or looser connection. She has loosened the connection and accepted the fact that Julie is making these plans. In the past, the connection between Julie's plans and Mom's management of them was tighter. For example, Mom may have done all the driving or arranged a ball game or a bowling outing. Now Julie is a teen, and the torque of the wrench is necessarily different. If it isn't, Julie will not learn how to pull friends together, make plans, and be accountable for her choices.

Often, it is not what we *don't* know that gets us into conflict with our teen; it is what we *think* we know and *believe* to be true. In other words, our assumptions are part of the issue. Not knowing is rarely the problem; knowing falsehoods are problematic.

When we adopt the belief that our perspective is the only one that counts, then we immediately close our mind to different views. (Remember the picture of the woman in Chapter 3, "Nuts and Bolts"?) In effect, we are not open to change. This kind of rigidity will ultimately alienate us from our teen.

Rules of Engagement

Control our Emotions

Try not to have a knee-jerk reaction, which is a biological, biochemical, and physiological reaction that distorts our judgment. If we choose to respond from this distorted, emotional place, we will make little progress and often inflame the situation.

We see red when we are upset. It is hard to be rational or stay calm in this mode, and we do not see much of anything else. When we are angry, scared, frustrated, or hurt, we say unhelpful and even detrimental words.

How do we step outside of the situation and respond to our teen less emotionally and more thoughtfully?

Spend More Time Being Silent While Our Teen is Talking

Teens expect us to react, resist, or attack ... *don't!* Many times, we are not truly listening to our teen. While the teen is speaking, we are talking in our own head, disagreeing with what's being said and formulating a response.

When we do this, we do not get a true sense of what he is trying to share. We can help our teen find the emotional literacy to better explain his thoughts, and help him articulate what he is feeling and what he needs (see "Stability: Encouraging Emotional Literacy" in Chapter 4, "The Level").

The result of not listening is that communication fails. Furthermore, each of us will end up feeling alienated and misunderstood, which only makes the situation with which we are dealing even more complicated.

Step Out to the Sidelines

When our teen speaks, we can remain quiet and try to listen. People yell because they think that no one is hearing them. Once someone feels heard, they will be more open to listening to what we want to say. We need to listen, paraphrase, ask if we understand correctly, and acknowledge opinions, feelings, and thoughts. This doesn't necessarily mean that we agree, but it does confirm that we are listening.

Separate the Doer from the Deed

When we listen, we may hear a scary plan, a dangerous idea, or something so vague—like "hanging out"—that we are unable to condone it. The teen is not bad or unacceptable; her plans, ideas, or behavioral choices are.

We want to avoid the pitfall of confusing the behavior with the person. Her list of possible plans and scary ideas, as well as her behavior, do not change who she is.

The best way to connect with our teen is by quiet listening. What is she feeling? What is she *really* saying? Do we understand what is bothering her? Once we can answer these questions, we are ready to start talking. When we show our teen the respect that we are truly listening, we have a good shot at having her actually listen to us!

If the Conversation is Not Going Well, Step Out of It

Reactional thinking (i.e., the urge to strike back, give in, or break off a discussion) is a signal to step out. Professional coaches stay out of the individual plays to keep their focus on the full field. If we lose our ability to be objective and understand the full situation, we are handicapping ourselves.

Write Things Down

While listening to our teen, we can take notes, which help us stay focused and not get too emotional. It is best when we are not drawn into the drama of the moment.

Make Relative Comments

Bringing in past situations is not always helpful. Other peoples' experiences do not always make things easier to understand. Avoid widening the battlefield with comments such as "When I was your age ..." and "Remember what happened to your cousin Sally ..."

Distinguish Negotiable from Nonnegotiable Issues

Every parent has nonnegotiable issues accompanied by varying levels of tolerance and acceptability for different behaviors. It is important that we take the time to recognize and share our feelings and beliefs with our teen. Sometimes we need to restate what seems obvious to us regarding education, health, safety, sex, language, religion, and morals.

Use a Team Approach

Instead of fighting each other, we need to be on the same team with our teens in order to collectively identify the issue and approach the problem. If we want to change their opinion, we need to understand it first. *If we can reposition the discussion and work with our teen to find a solution, we are far more likely to be successful.* The more things—even little things—on which we can agree, the easier it will be to tackle the bigger issues. Focusing on common ground is a good starting point.

For example, "The football team is doing well this year and the games are really exciting" or "I love Chinese food, too. It won't break your budget, so that's a great idea!" This type of dialogue shows respect and allows us to establish a more positive beginning with our teen. If we can actually agree on something—*anything*—it sets the tone in a positive light.

Zack has just asked Dad to use the car and Dad has said no.

Dad: You are a new driver and I don't like you just driving around.

Zack: You won't let me use the car. You are a *control freak*!

Here's another type of response:

Dad: Okay. You have your license now and you'd like to be able to take the car out. I understand that you want to have more independence. I am nervous because you do not have much experience driving, and I worry about careless mistakes and accidents. Even though I am nervous, I do think that you are good driver. Let's talk about when you want to use the car and where you want to go.

We can try to reposition the issue so that it is about safety and not control. The second response is an example of how Dad and Zack can come up with a plan that might work for both of them. Dad has loosened the torque a tiny bit—just enough for Zack to know that Dad is not a "control freak."

Clarify Needs and Goals

As we discussed in "Getting Connected by Listening and Communicating" (Chapter 3, "Nuts and Bolts") it is important to clarify needs and goals. If we say, "I'm confused. Let me see if I got this right," it allows us to paraphrase— or reflect—what our teenager has said and confirm that we understand him. It will also give him the opportunity to "correct" our understanding. In the process, he is learning to better explain his feelings and needs.

We need to clarify our own needs, expectations, and assumptions as well. If we are unclear, there is no way our teen can give us what we want. When searching for new solutions, we can begin by understanding what the both sides want. Let's revisit the Zack and Dad situation.

Zack: Well, it just seems like you don't trust me and you'll never let me go out with the car. What's the point of me sitting through all of those stupid Driver's Ed classes and getting my license if you don't let me use the car? It was all a waste of time! Everybody else gets to drive places, and I still have to hitch rides.

Dad: Yeah, I know the classes were boring, but it really helped bring down our insurance costs. I am little confused, though. Are you saying that you would have preferred not to get your license, or maybe you are embarrassed to ask for rides?

Zack: I am glad that I have my license, but it feels pointless not to be able to drive.

Dad: I never said that you couldn't drive at all.

Zack: It seems that way. Every time I ask, you say no.

Dad: Hmm. I agree that I have said no more times than I have said yes.

Zack: No kidding!

Dad: Okay, I get the point. You feel like you need more independence, and it seems to you that I am refusing to budge.

Zack: Bingo!

Dad: I am nervous about you driving because you don't have much experience. I also understand that you can't get experience unless you drive. Let's see if we can come up with some ideas that work. If you can be more specific about where you want to go, when you want to go, and with whom you might be, it would help me feel more comfortable.

As we tackle the rules of engagement (as discussed earlier in this chapter), it is necessary to keep ourselves open to changes and new possibilities. Learning to think outside the box and question the status quo are not easy skills. It helps to examine other perspectives. For example, when we see a traffic jam, our mind thinks of alternate routes that may get us to the same place. Just because one way of doing something works, it doesn't mean that there aren't other effective ways to handle an issue.

When we choose to "change the dance" or "change the route," we need to think through the consequences—the cause and effect of a choice—and truly "get" that they are connected. *When we choose a behavior, we choose the consequence.* The brainstorming part of this concept can give our teenager a sense of security, belonging, and maturity.

Remember to Be Nice

Name calling, put downs, and insults will never help resolve a conflict. If we catch ourselves behaving this way, we should step out.

Do Not Take One Another for Granted

Sometimes we treat strangers with more courtesy, respect, and appreciation than we do our children. On a regular basis, we should express appreciation, share a compliment, give a pleasant surprise, show affection, initiate a pleasant conversation, or give our complete attention to our teens.

Keep It Simple

The more specific we can be about what we want, the more likely it will be that we will get it. For example, asking our teen to clean up the kitchen is a very broad request. He may interpret those words as "putting the dishes in the sink" and "clearing off the counter." Instead, if we request that he unload the dishwasher, wipe down the counter, and sweep the floor, we are making a very clear request.

Avoid Ultimatums

Successful negotiations are based on compromises; conversely, ultimatums are power struggles where one person wins and the other loses.

Use "I" (Instead of "You") Statements

We can avoid using phrases such as "You betrayed my trust when you lied to me. You took the car without permission. You are so irresponsible." Instead, we can say, "I am so disappointed in your behavior tonight. I trusted you, and now that trust feels betrayed. I was so worried that something horrible might have happened. I was in a complete panic until I knew you were home and safe."

The key is to *avoid automatic emotional reactions*. We need to stop and try to discover the base issue. This effort will enable us to chart the course for the next step: *compromise.* Understanding conflict is an important opportunity to facilitate change. The tools used for the "rules of engagement" will create a foundation on which to build the "art of compromise."

CHAPTER 6

3-in-1 Oil

Problem Solving and the Art of Compromise

3-in-1 oil is a lubricant with thousands of uses, including getting unstuck. When families are caught in a conflict, everyone hurts. To avoid getting wedged in the middle of a disagreement, here are some very useful tools.

As parents, we have tools to prevent us from getting stuck in conflict. It is important to have the ability to loosen things up so we can find new solutions. These tools include problem solving and the wonderful art of compromise.

When we problem solve with our children, we are actually doing two things:

1. We are working out an issue (e.g., with homework or curfews); and

2. We are demonstrating a skill that will help our child be a more successful adult.

When we demonstrate that we can compromise, we show them that we know how to give a little here and there to get beyond a jam. We show our child that we can listen and take some responsibility for adjusting to a plan with good consequences. *Problem solving and compromise are about listening, self-responsibility, and consequences.*

Compromise is not a weakness. It is a process of give and take. It shows strength. Compromise is an opportunity to figure out what is important and allows for the most win-win opportunities. A win-win solution is a compromise that leaves everyone feeling like they are getting what they need most.

The ABCs: Keep Things Moving

How do we get flexibility when we approach a problem? Whether our approach is loud or quiet, fast or slow, gentle or direct, it always includes a chance to ask our teen about his view of the issue.

Here are the ABCs:

- **A**sk
- **B**rainstorm
- **C**hoose
- **D**o
- **E**valuate

All too often, parents and teens try to resolve different issues. If we attempt to dictate a solution, chances are that it will not work for long. Use the listening tools in the section entitled "Getting Connected by Listening and Communicating" (in Chapter 3, "Nuts and Bolts") to hear what our teen is concerned about and what he thinks is the actual issue.

Instead of engaging in a battle over every subject, consider going toe to toe on issues that have true significance, such as school, drugs, drinking, sex, or any health and safety concerns. Try not to get worked up about typical teenage phases, including odd clothes, strange hairstyles, or weird expressions. Adolescence can be draining, so we should try not to spend our energy on the smaller issues, and save it for when it truly matters.

We need to establish what we are willing to offer in order to get what we want. Everyone will feel more content with a solution that meets primary needs. This kind of problem solving is a creative process in which both the parent and the teenager participate. We can lead by example and teach the teen a vital skill. Problem solving is far more than just working out an issue, such as homework or curfews. This ability will help our teen become a more successful adult.

Teens want to feel self-sufficient and accomplished. We need to learn not to overprotect our children and instead allow them to begin to manage for themselves. If we solve their problems for them, how will they learn to resolve their own? Ultimately, compromise allows for win-win opportunities.

Watch Zach and his dad benefit from using the ABCs as Zack is heading out the door.

Zack: See ya, Dad. I'll be home at midnight.

Dad: No. Home at 10 tonight.

Zack: Dad, don't be ridiculous! I have stuff to do tonight.

Dad: Well, I can't be up until all hours waiting for you to come home!

Ask

Asking questions helps us figure out what is truly important to ourselves and to our kids. Is the real issue about meeting curfew, swearing, getting good grades, working, going to a party, or making the team?

We need to learn to identify and clarify a problem once we realize that something is wrong. Collecting as much information and as many facts as possible will help define the situation.

Zack: But Dad, you don't understand!

Dad: Okay, maybe I don't. Can you explain it to me?

These are helpful questions to establish the unmet need:

- "What is it that you want?"
- "Why is this important to you?"
- "What are the consequences for you if it doesn't happen or you don't get it?"

- "What is the impact to me or to our family?"

Zack: Well, I kind of have a date with this new girl, Lisa. We are going to the movies with Bill and Ruth. Bill doesn't have a car tonight, so I said I'd drive. It is a 9:15 movie and, by the time it gets out and I drive everybody home, it'll be close to midnight before I get home.

Dad: I understand your timing issue. My concern is that I do not go to sleep until you are home safe and sound. Also, I just got a call from work and they need me to come in for a double shift tomorrow. So, before I leave in the morning, I have to feed the horses and fix the barn door for the hay delivery. I am tired already.

Zack: I didn't know that. You have been working a lot this week. Lisa is so cool. I can't believe that she actually said she'd go to the movie with me! She is friendly with Ruth, so I think that helps. I'd feel like a real idiot if I had to cancel out on everyone.

It is helpful to define what the teen really wants (e.g., the cool factor, independence, or freedom) and to know what is important for us (e.g., not worrying, health and safety, or a good night's sleep). Understanding how to resolve conflict begins with asking.

We need to try and get as many of the details established as we can before we react. Once we think that we have a good feel for the situation, we can start to brainstorm.

Brainstorm

Brainstorming is important in order to develop a number of options for a given problem. We can list all of the ideas that we and our teen have thought of, but we should not evaluate them yet. We don't want to stop the creative juices from flowing because the last idea may be the best solution! Write them all down—from the simple and easy options to the complicated and challenging ones. Even bad ideas have a place on the list.

Together, Zack and Dad will try to find a solution or a compromise with which they can each live. Teens relish the idea that they helped craft a plan; it gives them a sense of ownership in the solution. The goal is for each to get something they want or need.

When we ask our teen to help us understand why this is important to him, it helps shift the focus to working together to solve a common problem. Ask for their ideas. People see things differently when they are involved in the process.

With a touch of humor, in a joint effort, here's an example:

Dad: How about not going out at all tonight? Invite the gang over and watch a movie here. I'll make the popcorn.

Zack: Yeah, right. That'd be *way* loads of fun! Maybe I could double check with Bill and see if Ruth can get a car.

Dad: You could see if they can go to an earlier movie.

Zack: Dad, what if I get the barn chores done for you in the morning? That way, you could sleep later and go straight to work.

Choose

Now is the time to discuss each potential solution and identify the most probable outcomes for each option. Consider the positive and negative outcomes as well as the long- and short-term consequences.

- Does this option meet the basic needs of both people?
- Can you both live with this solution?
- Is this a realistic expectation?

Dad: Zack, that is a *great* idea. I don't usually feed the horses until 7 or 7:30. I was feeding them early because I had to leave for work by 7. Why don't you call me when the movie is over and you are heading home? Then I will get ready for bed so I can turn in as soon as you are home.

Zack: Sure, I can do that.

Problem solving is a creative process that allows both parent and teenager to get out of a stuck spot. *A problem is an opportunity to demonstrate the techniques of working things out.* Problem solving includes an attitude of curiosity and creativity.

Now that Dad and Zack have gone through the ABCs (**A**sk, **B**rainstorm, and **C**hoose), it is time to advance to **D** and **E** (**Do** and **Evaluate**).

Do

Once we have chosen a solution, we must determine if it is doable. Here, we place emphasis on the need to review and try again if the solution does not feel achievable. Determining this ahead of time helps us be more realistic and perhaps optimistic about finding effective solutions to problems.

This is a good time to make concrete plans for carrying out the solution and acknowledge that it may take more than one try to find the best one.

Zack: I think this is a good idea.

Dad: Let's see how it goes for the weekend. It might be a good way to handle this at other times when I need to go into work early.

Evaluate

Establish a time to review the effectiveness of the choice. Maybe it is a week, or perhaps a month, but set aside some time to look at how it is going.

- Has the situation improved?
- Has the original conflict relaxed?
- Is it still there?
- Has it been redirected?

Take a close look. Be open to adjusting something and trying again. This is an ongoing process.

Here's what happened after the weekend:

Dad: Let's talk about how our solution worked out this weekend. It was certainly nice for me to get a good night's sleep.

Zack: Yeah, it was okay. I am glad that I was able to drive everyone home. I didn't love getting up so early, but I'd do it again if I can have another date with Lisa!

Dad: Glad to hear the date went well. How was the movie?

It is also important to be aware of barriers or challenges to communicating well. While we have pointed out the importance of asking questions and making sure that we have as much information and facts as possible, it is also important to avoid distractions (e.g., the telephone, TV, noise, and multitasking).

It is good to communicate when there is plenty of time, not when there is only 10 minutes left before leaving. Remember to let go of preconceived perceptions. In the beginning, we need to be open and neutral if we truly want to understand what is happening. Swearing rarely helps!

Mom and Sam have been battling over the messiness of Sam's bedroom and the family room. Both are rooms in which Sam spends a lot of his time, and both rooms are in continual disarray. Mom is getting very frustrated with picking up after Sam.

Here is a typical conversation:

Mom: Sam, how many times do I have to ask you not to leave your socks and shoes in the middle of the family room? You also left dishes in your bedroom. I can't stand it when you eat upstairs!

Sam: What's the big deal? It's not like a crime or anything!

Mom: You think things are cleaned up by magic? I pick up after you all of the time.

Let's try a different approach:

Mom: Sam, can we talk for a minute?

Sam: I guess so.

Mom: You know how it bugs me to clean up after you in the family room, and how I am always after you to keep your bedroom in better shape?

Sam: Yeah, it's kind of obvious. I hate it when you nag me about stuff.

Mom: Neither of us likes it very much. I was wondering if we could try and work something out that we can both live with.

Sam: Okay …

Mom: What do you think would be a reasonable expectation for your bedroom?

Sam: Um, that you never come in my room and I can keep it however I want?

Again, remember that humor can be helpful:

Mom: How about if you make your bed every day, don't leave clothes on the floor, and don't eat on your bed?

Sam: I could just close my door …

Mom: Well, at least I wouldn't have to look at your typhoon of a bedroom!

Sam: What if I cleaned my room once a week?

Mom: Define "clean."

Sam: Bed made, clothes put away, no dishes in my room … and I'll close my door during the week so you don't have to look at my beloved typhoon!

Mom: Let's give that a try for two weeks and see how it goes. I won't bug you about your room as long as you show me once a week that it is picked up and clean.

We are trying to find a common ground with which we can all live. We are establishing what we need because we won't get what we do not ask for. We are choosing our battles and showing that we can be flexible.

Likewise, our teen needs to get a handle on what is important to them, too. They will begin to learn that there are different ways of handling conflict, and that conflict can sometimes bring them to a better place of understanding.

Let's Make a Deal

Sometimes the art of compromise means that we need to step out of a discussion or argument and rechart our course:

- We need to make sure that we are on the right path and are going in the best direction.
- We need to embrace the idea that the goal is to find a common agreement.
- Through mutual understanding, each of us might give up something in order to create a larger gain.
- The process of the collaboration is crucial to a successful outcome.

Both sides need to feel that they have helped craft the solution. Instead of thinking about the issue as "adult against teen," it will help to view it as "adult and teen figuring out how to deal with this challenge." This team approach is certainly more likely to result in an agreement and a plan that each can accept and that has a good chance of succeeding.

Here is a dialog between Annie and Dad, who have a recurring battle over how Annie should spend her time on school nights.

Dad: So, Annie, how much homework do you have tonight?

Annie: Are you going to start bugging me about my priorities again?

Dad: I am just trying to help. You know that you will accomplish more if you do one thing at a time and really focus.

Annie: No, Dad. *You* accomplish more when *you* do one thing at a time. My grades are fine.

Dad: They could be better if you had more discipline. Besides, when you take all night to do stuff, you stay up too late and then you are impossible to wake up in the morning. You need an earlier bedtime. You missed the bus twice last week and I had to drive you to school! That's not very responsible.

Annie: Dad, please just back off!

Dad: No, I don't think you get it. I know that when you are on the computer, you are also on Facebook. How can you concentrate on your U.S. history term paper?

Annie: Well, I do.

Dad: It just seems like you never manage your time well enough.

A version of this conversation happens several times a week. Annie and Dad are stuck, so let's try some 3-in-1 "compromise" oil. It also helps to remember to avoid the phrases "You always" and "You never."

Dad: Annie, I feel like I have been nagging you a lot lately about how you spend your time and about not getting to bed at a decent hour. I don't like feeling like I am a broken record. I want to try something different.

Annie: Are you for real?

Dad: I was thinking that, in less than two years, you will be away at college and you will not have the pleasure of constant loving guidance ... seriously, I want you to become responsible to *yourself* for the things that you need to do. I guess I am also realizing that we may do things differently.

Annie: Now I *know* you are crazy! Who are you and what did you do with my father?

Dad: I know this is very different than what I usually say, but what I usually say wasn't getting us anywhere. I want to wipe the slate clean and not talk about old stuff. Here are my thoughts: I want the best for you and I want you to have as many options as possible.

Annie: Well, the same with me.

Dad: Good. We are agreeing on something already! I think that you do not get enough sleep. I know that when I stay up too late, I pay for it the next day. I also tend to go to bed earlier the next night so I can catch up on my sleep. Truly, though, you need to figure that out for yourself.

Annie: So what are you saying?

Dad: I think you should be in charge of your evening and your bedtime, but we need to agree on the expectations. As long as you maintain a B average (or stay on honor roll) and don't miss the bus in the morning, I won't bug you.

Annie: What happens if I oversleep?

Dad: Well, it makes me late for work when I have to drive you to school. The whole idea is that you are responsible for yourself. How would you get to school if I weren't here?

Annie: I would have to walk, and that would take 45 minutes. I'd be even later for class. Could we make a deal?

Dad: Let's hear it.

Annie: As long as I don't oversleep more than twice a month, could you give me a ride? If I mess up more than twice, I walk.

Dad: I would be willing to work with that. Let's see how it works for the next month.

Annie: Thanks, Dad!

Annie and Dad have become unstuck. They have loosened up enough to try something different. This may or may not be the compromise that works, but they have shown each other that they are willing to work at it and experiment with different ways of handling the situation. They are learning that they can talk through an issue and come up with alternatives. This is a win-win situation.

We need to figure out what we need (e.g., grades, chores, or time) and specifically ask for it. If we can agree on a common goal, we are off to a great start. Our teen may choose a different path to this goal, but that is part of their learning curve. We can discuss the alternatives and consequences.

A compromise shows respect for someone else and permits both parties to get what they truly need. We may give up our specific ideas of how to do this, or even have less significant needs met, but we are making progress.

Learning to solve problems creatively is a skill that will continually help our teen throughout life and come in handy in school, work, and play. It is vital to remember that *problem solving is about listening for the true issues, being responsible for ourselves, and understanding the positive and negative consequences of our choices.*

Teens need to figure this out. They need to experience self-sufficiency and realize that they *can* resolve issues.

CHAPTER 7

The Measuring Tape

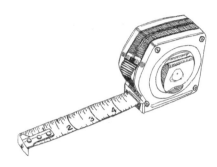

Having, Losing, and Regaining Trust

The only way to make a man trustworthy is to trust him.
~Henry Stimson

A measuring tape allows us to calibrate the tiniest positive movements in a given situation or response. It reminds us that things change an inch at a time. Trust is a great example of things changing one step (or inch) at a time. How do we establish—or reestablish—trust? We certainly know when it is gone, yet we don't always know how to get it back.

Healthy parenting, and teaching, are about compassion and forgiveness. We want to raise children in an environment of support and acceptance. We want to communicate to them that everyone makes mistakes and that, when mistakes are made, *forgiveness is available.*

Forgiveness is a critically important part of the learning process; however:

- Forgiveness does not mean that we accept all of our teenager's misbehaviors without saying anything.

- Forgiveness does not mean that we do not discipline our teen.

- Forgiveness does not mean that we can't get angry with our teen's behavior and choices.

This is worth repeating: *Raising children can be one of the most emotionally evocative and stressful experiences in our lives.* There will always be times when our teen pushes our buttons and we might respond in less-than-productive ways; however, we can discipline ourselves so that we remember to respond to our children with support and compassion.

We need to assure our teens that our forgiveness is available and their lovability is intact. This is a crucial step in creating and recreating trust.

Here are some measures we can take to inch our way back to trust:

- Separate the teen from their behavior.

- Forgive them and show compassion.

- Offer the gift of responsibility.

- Catch them doing it right.

- Set boundaries and expectations ahead of time.

Separate the Teen from Their Behavior

Mom and Charlie are arguing. Mom has just discovered that Charlie lied about his plans for the evening: He was not at the movies but was instead at an unchaperoned party.

Mom: That's *it*, Charlie! You are grounded for two months!

Charlie: It's not such a big deal. You are overreacting, as always.

Mom: I just can't trust you. You did not do what you told me you were going to do. You out and out lied to me. How can I trust *anything* you ever say to me? I will never know if I can believe you again. You are such a liar!

Mom is feeling hurt and angry, as if Charlie pulled the rug out from under her. As adults, we know that people make poor choices, which can challenge relationships, and it can be very hard to reestablish the stability that comes with trust. Trust is an intangible, immeasurable concept; therefore, earning *and* giving it can be difficult.

Avoid statements such as "You are untrustworthy" or "You are unreliable." Instead, try comments like "I am disappointed in the choice you made tonight. How can I trust your decision-making abilities?"

In our teen's search for independence, we (teens and parents) sometimes confuse trust for love, and then take our teen's deception personally. *Our love is a constant force.* Few things would convince a parent to stop loving their child, which is a characteristic of parenting; however, we do not always have trust. Trust in our teen—and their trust in us—are usually hard won.

It is the teen's job to push the boundaries as he figures out how to be an independent person. Charlie probably knew that he shouldn't have done what he did because he lied about it. Perhaps he did not feel that he could explain the party to his mom, or perhaps he knew that attending this party was completely against the rules.

Mom: We need to figure out how to do this differently. I don't want to be the parent who always has to worry about whether or not my kid is being truthful. You are a good kid and I want to be able to trust what you are telling me. Even though I may not like *what* you're telling me, I want you to feel like you can tell me what's going on. I know kids have parties and they drink. That doesn't mean that I think it's okay for you to go to parties and get into mischief, but I am not naïve.

Charlie: So if I had told you about the party, you would have let me go?

Mom: Maybe and maybe not. We may have needed to come up with a compromise. Maybe you could've gone for an hour or two. I don't know what I would've said, but you never gave me—or us—a chance to figure that out.

Charlie: Really?

Mom: Charlie, I like trusting you. Being able to trust you is very important to me. You and I get along better when we trust each other, don't we? Things are just easier. I do not like having to second-guess what you tell me. I am willing to talk about trying different ways of doing this.

In the above response, Mom is giving Charlie important messages about building bridges and compromising.

Forgive Them and Show Compassion

Sometimes our teen's behavior and the situation they present are more challenging. There might be an ongoing pattern where the distrust runs deep and wide. We may get backed into a corner and have a hard time digging ourselves out.

Dad has just discovered that Steve continued to be on the Internet while grounded from being online for using it inappropriately.

Dad: I cannot *believe* that you did this again! Nothing ever changes with you. How can I have faith in any conversation we have? You completely disrespect me. I am *sick* of it!

Steve: You just like to have things your way all of the time. You don't get me. You think you know how it is all supposed to be. You never listen to me!

Dad: Well, I certainly listened to you when you agreed not to use the Internet for two weeks … and what did you just do?

Steve: That was *your* idea, not mine.

Dad: Well, obviously, your word never means anything and I can never expect you to follow through on anything. You are basically worthless!

Steve: So what's the point in even *talking* about this?

Compassion includes the ability to forgive. How much compassion can we muster up when our teens stumble and fall? Withholding forgiveness causes shame.

Shame carries the message that we've done something terribly wrong. In fact, our transgression is so terrible that it is beyond forgiveness. *Shame is transmitted when a parent refuses to forgive a child.* Without forgiveness, there is no hope or opportunity for growth and change. With no chance of change, we are truly stuck.

Dad: Steve, I am so disappointed that you chose to ignore our agreement of not going on the Internet for two weeks. I feel sad and angry that this has happened again.

Steve: It's just not that simple. *Everything* is online. It's like not being able to breathe. You just don't get it.

Dad: Perhaps I don't get it. My world does not revolve around the Internet. What I do get is that you are a good kid but sometimes the Internet takes over. You spend hours and hours lost on your computer, and it concerns your mom and me. We miss you. We like spending time with you and hearing about what is going on.

Steve: Well, I use it for school, too, you know.

Dad: Yes, we know that, but you do way more than schoolwork online. Remember that is what got us into this situation in the first place!

Steve: I said I was sorry. I didn't realize that downloading that game would put a virus on the computer, and I really didn't know that the other site was a porn site.

Dad: I forgive you for making those mistakes. I believe you when you said that you did not do it intentionally. I understand that sometimes things can just happen. Even though I got very mad, I don't think that you did it to get back at me. This doesn't mean that it is okay, but it does mean that I know you are not a bad person.

Steve: So you accept my apology?

Dad: Yes. The problem that I have is that you chose to disregard the grounding from the Internet. That just made the situation worse. I wish you had talked to me about it rather than sneak around and do it anyway. It just makes it harder for me to trust what you are saying.

Offer the Gift of Responsibility

Part of reestablishing trust is to be able to show responsibility. When our teen has lied about where they have been or what they have or have not done, we need to show them the road back to trustworthiness.

If we can help our teen learn that the first step to regain trust is to take responsibility for their actions, and then provide opportunities for them to show responsibility, we are moving in the right direction. This can help us let go of our own hurt and anger when they have disappointed us. Asking teens to be responsible is a gift from us to them.

Dad: Do you understand why we got so upset about this Internet thing?

Steve: I guess. I mean I should be more careful about what I download. I need to make sure that it is safe. I know I spend a lot of time online talking with my friends.

Dad: Anything else?

Steve: I kind of let you guys down by going behind your back. Now you won't trust me about anything.

Dad: It sounds like you understand why we got so mad. It is also important that you know that, even though you let us down, we still love you. We want to trust you, so let's work on a plan. We need to trust that you will do what you say you are going to do. We are going to start with small, specific things.

Steve: Okay …

Once our teen has understood why the trust was mislaid, they can take the first step and own their part of the responsibility. The second step is to find opportunities to follow through and do what he says he is going to do.

Teens are literal. We can help provide a road map by creating chores and jobs that will give them the opportunity to show that they can be trusted. These may be small things, such as taking out the garbage, unloading the dishwasher, or babysitting for a younger sibling. They may be things that we never thought of as "trust" issues, but they are the building blocks that will help us see our teen as trustworthy and our teen recognize that he can be trusted.

Catch Them Doing It Right

Reliability is a version of trustworthiness, and we need to be aware of the small and large steps. When we notice our teen's behavior and actions changing, we need to make sure that we acknowledge the positive changes.

If we continue to expect the same behavior from our teen, it does not give him the opportunity to begin to get it right.

It is important to notice positive moments, and then comment on it. It may be little things at first, such as:

- "Thanks for clearing the table."
- "You did a nice job."
- "Thanks for taking the garbage out."

- "It was nice having you home for dinner."
- "Your sister loved having you watch TV with her."
- "I appreciate your coming home on time."

We need to remind them that the little things matter and add up. It also helps to remind us that our teens are capable, good, and worth trusting again.

Set Boundaries and Expectations Ahead of Time

Even though we are discussing this last, setting boundaries is something to think about ahead of time. In moments of calmness, when there are no pressing issues, it is good to talk about trust. We often do not recognize the immense value trust holds until we have lost it. We need to have conversations with our teens about what trust means and why it is so important.

Discuss the consequences of not being able to trust what someone says, and describe what a scary place that might be. This is also the time to remind our teen that there is forgiveness and the opportunity to get back on track.

Dad: Hey, Steve, have you got some time? I'd like to have one of those father–son talks.

Steve: Ah, Dad, you told me about the birds and the bees in seventh grade!

Dad: No birds and bees, I promise, although this is important, too. I know that you are growing up and have a lot of new and different choices in front of you. I also know how much I value being able to talk with you, and how deeply I trust your choices.

Steve: Oh, is this a health and safety chat?

Dad: Well, kind of. I was reading an article in the paper about the kids who were in that bad car accident on Monday night and I got to thinking. Your mom and I need to feel comfortable that you are safe.

Steve: Dad, you know that I won't do anything stupid!

Dad: I believe that you would not intentionally do something stupid, but we all make mistakes. I want you to know that I will always love you—even if I am really mad. I will never stop loving you.

Steve: Are you going soft on me?

Dad: No, I am being serious. I want to be clear with you. I expect you to be where you say you are going to be. I expect you to do what you say you are going to do. I expect you to be straight with me. In return, I will be straight with you. If we get off track and lose this mutual respect and trust, we will have to go back to square one.

Steve: Sort of like when I was a kid and you checked up on me all of the time?

Dad: Yes, and we'd go back to earlier curfews and limiting activities. We'd have to slowly create opportunities for you to earn back the responsibility so you could be more independent again.

Steve: I get it, Dad.

Dad: I like that we can have a mature conversation. Does this seem fair to you?

Steve: Yeah. I like that you and Mom trust me, and I like being able to do stuff.

Dad: Thanks for talking this through with me.

These simple steps lay the groundwork for future situations. *When we can be clear and concrete with our expectations, we are more likely to get and maintain what we need: trust with our teen.* Through this trust, our teen is better able to become the responsible young adult we want him to be.

Good judgment comes from experience,
and experience comes from bad judgment!
~ Anonymous

CHAPTER 8

The Screwdriver

Discipline: Lefty Lucy, Righty Tighty

A screwdriver tightens and relaxes a connection, which is similar to our approach for discipline. The concept of discipline can be frightening and overwhelming. We don't want to be too strict or harsh, yet we don't want to relinquish our parental authority and responsibility to keep our sons and daughters safe.

The keys to successful discipline are clarity, consistency, predictability, and compassion. We want to keep our kids healthy and safe while they pursue their impending young adult independence.

We need to be clear with ourselves and our teens about our disciplinary goals. *Discipline is an opportunity for a correction.* It should not be about control because, ultimately, we don't have total command over our teen's world. In addition, we are trying to help instill in teens a means of cultivating their own internal self-discipline—not ours.

The question that we need to ask ourselves is, "When is our teen ready for certain privileges, responsibilities, and activities?" This includes dating, socializing, driving, working, traveling, and curfews. This is an individual decision for each of us to make based on our family values and our teen's maturity level.

A teen's desire to belong, his quest for knowledge, and growing independence are examples of influences beyond our control. Therefore, self-discipline is better than parental discipline because we eventually want him to learn to be responsible.

Discipline is always a work in progress. The limits we set at 16 years of age may not be appropriate at 17. We need to remember that *we create rules to keep our children safe and to teach them to develop their own boundaries.*

Discipline, like a screwdriver, is a tool that can go to the right or the left and can tighten or loosen. Our job is to know when to tighten and loosen the grip.

Here are some tools, skills, and guidelines that can help us with discipline:

- Make agreements and establish rules.

- Be consistent, show respect, and treat our teen fairly.

- Keep the discussions short.

- Use humor and be positive when possible.

- If it's not working, try something new.

The latest research in the fields of behavioral modification, cognitive behavioral psychology, and social psychology—as well as advancements in neuroscience and studies of human nature[1]—tells us that behavior can be changed. *This is good news!*

We need to find the best ways to help jump start behavioral change. As parents and teachers, we have the right and the responsibility to guide our teen's behavior. We want to encourage behavior that we desire.

Sometimes, teens do not fully understand, or are unaware of, the behavior that we dislike, such as talking back, swearing, answering evasively, and leaving dishes or clothes around the house. We need to be painfully clear about what we want by stating our basic expectations. Nothing is too simple or too obvious.

In working with teens, I have found that they will respond to limits and consequences. *We use limits and rules to strengthen our impact on their behavior.* After we discipline them, we watch to see that they behave, and then we slowly loosen the grip. Later, teens will begin to test the boundaries again, which means that we need to keep that screwdriver handy, just in case.

We should not be surprised if our teen is manipulative. Accept that they will try to get away with whatever they can because, in a sense, it is their "job" in becoming an adult to test their own abilities and figure out the cause and effect of their choices and actions. It is our "job" to set consistent guidelines and consequences for breaking rules.

Make Agreements and Establish Rules

There are certainly nonnegotiable rules (e.g., for health and safety) and each family will determine their own. We need to choose these rules carefully and explain them to our teen. By doing so, we are sharing our morals and establishing a basic set of agreements. *Agreements encourage responsibility.*

Creating an agreement begins with a discussion about expectations (e.g., expectations regarding car use, grades, chores, volunteer work, and sports). If we can create a common goal, then we can begin to figure out how to achieve it.

Once we can declare what each of us needs to do, and define the positive and negative consequences, we can create an agreement. This is similar to the concepts in "Problem Solving and the Art of Compromise" (Chapter 6, "3-in-1 Oil") and "Having, Losing, and Regaining Trust" (Chapter 7, "The Measuring Tape").

By establishing agreements and rules ahead of time, as Mom is doing with Mary in the example below, we are instilling self-discipline.

Mary knows the consequences of not following rules because Mom has begun a conversation about this with Mary at the beginning of high school—*before* there are any problems. Together, they have begun to go over their separate expectations. Mary will be making behavioral choices and, because she knows the rules, these will be informed choices.

Mom: Mary, got a few minutes? I want to talk with you about the next school year. High school is going to be very different from middle school.

Mary: Mom, you are weird!

Mom: I know, but I want to set some boundaries ahead of time.

Mary: I am not a bad kid, and I don't get in trouble, so what are you worried about?

Mom: It's not so much that I am worried, but I want us to be prepared. These things may never be an issue but, if they are, we will both have a better understanding of what to do.

Be Consistent, Show Respect, and Treat Teens Fairly

Mom has entered into a conversation that will cover different factors over many weeks and months. We will identify some of these factors next because knowing how to recognize them will help us evaluate how Mom and Mary are doing in their talk.

Consistency needs to be fair and respectful. We also need to be specific about our expectations and the consequences.

To be effective, *discipline needs to be dependable and make sense.* The intent should not be to embarrass or punish. It may help to discover what is behind the misbehavior in order to choose the correct disciplinary reaction:

- Is our teen looking for attention, control, revenge, or independence?

- Is this a display of inadequacy, excitement, or peer acceptance?

- Are they overwhelmed or out of control?

Consider this: If one teen is acting out because he wants our attention and needs us to be more involved, and another is rebelling because of her desire for more independence, then their needs—and thus our responses—would be very different. This may give us important information about how to move forward. Another consideration is to determine the person being affected by the situation, as it will help us choose the best response:

- Has our teen's choice affected us or someone else (e.g., not feeding the dog, being hurtful, leaving a bike in the driveway, or driving recklessly)?

- Is it a self-focused problem (e.g., not doing homework, staying up too late, or not doing laundry)?

The concept of fairness is very important to teens. Setting consequences ahead of time is a helpful way to be fair. This practice ensures that we make choices rationally. If our teen drives too fast, they know they may get a ticket; if they are late for school, they know they will receive detention. The punishment, or the consequence, should make sense for the infraction. Likewise, we should take the time to predetermine the consequences for certain behaviors, such as getting home late, getting poor grades, not doing chores, or lying.

Mom and Mary can discuss specific issues, such as parties, dating, curfews, grades, lying, and chores, and jointly talk about the consequences for poor choices. They can predetermine what happens if she does not do her laundry, comes home late, or doesn't do her homework. This creates a sense of fairness because Mary will know and understand the consequences of her choices.

This brings us to the matter of respect. When a situation occurs for which we are not prepared (and it will!), we will need spontaneous discipline. *For discipline to be successful, respect is required.*

Listening and understanding both sides of the story are important skills (see "Getting Connected by Listening and Communicating" in Chapter 3, "Nuts and Bolts"). If we want our teens to listen to us, we need to hear them as well. Yelling and name calling are not respectful. Both sides need to be able to trust that neither side will hurt the other.

- *Be clear.* Make sure we ask for what we want and that our expectations are understandable.

- *Be fair.* The punishment should fit the crime. Talk about consequences ahead of time.

- *Be sensitive.* Know that the behavior was stupid, not the teen.

- *Be loving.* Touch her and remind her that we love her.

- *Be focused.* Don't wash the dishes or talk on the phone while we are disciplining our child.

- *Be firm.* Once we have made a rule, don't change it for the sake of quiet or peace. Routine and order are important.

- *Keep our cool, and try not to respond to anger with anger.* Don't impose consequences when we are still angry because this can be overbearing. Make sure the consequence is logical and doable.

When we use "grounding" for everything, we are missing an opportunity to teach our teen an appropriate lesson. As an example, if our boss docked our lunch hour because we messed up a presentation to a client, would that make sense? We would not have learned anything except to be afraid of the boss's power. If the boss directs us to a better understanding of the facts that we didn't present, we would learn something valuable for the next presentation.

The aim of discipline should be to create a scenario where our teen learns from her behavior; otherwise, we are all trapped in a continuous cycle.

Keep It Short

When making a correction, keep it simple and brief. There is no need for a long, in-depth discussion. Explain specifically what she has done and exactly how we feel about it. *Don't attack her; instead, focus on the disappointing behavior or choice.*

Remind her that we love her and reiterate the many things she does well. Make contact, such as a hand on her shoulder or knee. We need to make a point and move on. She heard us—even if she pretends that she didn't. Less is more.

Mom: I am angry, upset, and hurt because the choice you made tonight scared … worried … disrespected … our relationship and me. It put you in danger. As you know, you will not be allowed to drive the car, go out on a school night, or sleep over at a friend's house for two weeks.

Now, turn the corner. We have delivered the message of our anger and disappointment, so we can add the following:

Mom: I know you are capable of better decisions. You choose to do many things well, and I respect you for those decisions. I love you. Nothing will change that.

Then, touch her on the shoulder and leave. *Our statements will have much more effect if we avoid repeating ourselves and do not fall into a back-and-forth conversation.* Stating our opinion often doesn't convince them; their experiences teach them a better lesson.

Keep it Positive and Use Humor

We need to catch our teen doing things right, even if it is only half-right. *We need to tell them specifically what they did that we liked and how it made us feel.* We can challenge ourselves to catch them being good three to five times a day.

Discipline does not always have to be serious, so use humor. Here are a few ideas that might help get our message across without sounding too harsh or critical. These are silly ideas, yet they can have an impact without making us feel like a nag. The next time our teen answers a question with a shoulder shrug, we can try putting our fingers on our forehead and saying any of the following statements:

- "Hold on! I am receiving an ESP message. You would like a cheeseburger for dinner!"

- "Hmm, I am sensing that you put your little brother up for adoption!"

- Put a note on the clothes on the floor, which says, "Please hang me up so you don't step on me!" or "Am I clean or dirty?"

- Put a note on the towel on the floor, which says, "Please hang me up so I don't smell bad" or "I miss my friend, the washcloth. Can you bring me back to the bathroom?"

Improvement and effort can be rewarded. Even if the end goal is not achieved, progress can function as encouragement to keep going. *When we stay positive, we increase the chances that they'll change their behavior.* Make eye contact and clearly state what we want. Be direct and concrete. Once we see the behavior that we desire, we need to make sure that we acknowledge it.

If It's Not Working, Try Something New

We should try to avoid power struggles because they are not about problem solving; they are about winning. *Discipline is not about winning; it is about safety.* It is crucial for us to acknowledge that, if what we are doing is not working, then we need to do something different.

Perhaps grounding has no effect, threats are meaningless, punishments aren't working, and lectures fall on deaf ears. "Been there, done that" shows us that we need to be open to change. There is no "one size fits all" approach.

It may be more effective to let him experience the natural or logical consequences of the situation than try to make him do something because we dictate it. *When we force an action, we will often get rebellion, revenge, sneakiness, and resentment in return.*

Recognizing that we need to try something different can be hard, but it can also be enlightening. Talk with a friend, spouse, or colleague; recheck our perspective; think about what we are hoping to accomplish.

Review "Getting Connected by Listening and Communicating" (Chapter 3, "Nuts and Bolts") and "Problem Solving and the Art of Compromise" (Chapter 6, "3-in-1 Oil"). We may have missed some important information.

Remember that discipline is a correction. *We are seeking improved behavior.* A "disconnected" punishment won't foster growth and improvement. If we put our teen on the defensive, we are apt to destroy their motivation to try something different.

Solely pointing out shortfalls is dangerous. Constructive criticism is risky. *We do not want our teen to be changing their behavior because we have criticized it.* We want our teen to understand how and why changing their behavior might be better.

We want to encourage our teen's ability to make safe, healthy decisions using their own developing self-discipline. We need to nurture their sense of self-discipline and encourage a deepening of their common sense. This is a crucial step in our teen's maturation. Self-reflection, understanding consequences, and making better choices for themselves is important.

ENDNOTE

1. Michael S. Gazzaniga, *The Cognitive Neurosciences,* 4th edition (Cambridge, MA: The MIT Press, 2009).

CHAPTER 9

The Glue

Self-esteem and Self-confidence:
The Stuff That Holds It All Together

Glue is the sticky stuff that holds things together. Self-esteem and self-confidence, like glue, are the substances that hold us together when things fall apart.

In order to build our teen's self-confidence, and help them feel good about themselves, we can catch them when they do things right. If we notice the little things they do well, and emphasize their positive behaviors, actions, and accomplishments, they will get the message that we admire them for who they are and want to acknowledge them for what they do.

Encouraging self-confidence in our teens requires a great deal of sensitivity on our part. Before we open our mouth, we might want to think about how the teen will likely respond to our words. We can ask ourselves, "What do I want my teen to learn from this interaction?"

Teens need to feel responsible and accountable. When we give our teens reasonable responsibility, they feel trusted, competent, and respected. We can provide opportunities for them to do well at age-appropriate practical tasks. They need to learn the methods that lead to success as well as know how to deal with frustration when they fail. Their common sense will develop through relevant and practical experiences.

Here's how we encourage self-esteem and self-confidence:

- Use praise.
- Be real and specific about expectations.
- Use constructive criticism.
- Use encouragement.
- Teach self-reliance.
- Anticipate failures.
- Inspire without pressure.

When possible, we want to find the moments that allow our teen to feel good. We want to approve of and accept who he is. We want him to be comfortable with his own self-image. We wish for our teens to have self-acceptance.

This is the road to independence, which is vital for growing up. Developing pride in one's competence, experiencing challenges and surviving them, experimenting with risks and different ways of doing things, gaining control over what happens, and learning to set boundaries are all essential tools in becoming an autonomous and responsible adult.

Use Praise

While the use of praise is merited in many situations, we need to be aware of how we use it. *Praise, to be meaningful, needs to be real.* Of course, there are times when a "Certificate of Participation" is appropriate, but, if we are striving to have our teens be independent, self-aware, and achieving people, we need them to understand what it takes to accomplish a project or task.

Praise, when misapplied, may backfire by teaching our teen that he needs our approval or recognition in order to be successful. It is important for him to comprehend that he needs to have self-appreciation for "a job well done." We want him to be proud of himself. This results in self-esteem, which will keep him from falling apart when life gets challenging.

Dad: You make me so proud! It makes me so happy when you do well.

Steven: Thanks, Dad!

In this exchange, Dad is trying to use praise, but he left out a few important details. He is talking about how *he* feels, not about how *his son* feels. Does Dad really want his son to do well to please him? Steven may continue to seek his father's approval for his choices and successes.

While it feels good when they consult us, *we want our teens to internalize self-approval.* We want them to be able to find encouragement from within and not rely on others. Similar to the concept of self-discipline (discussed in Chapter 8, "The Screwdriver"), being able to feel approval from within is a huge step towards growing up.

Here is another way that Dad could respond:

Dad: It must have felt so good for you to have aced the test! You worked hard and you deserve that grade.

or:

Dad: What a nice recognition you received from the coach (or boss or teacher). You should be very proud of yourself. I am so pleased for you.

The message is similar but, instead of us "owning" a piece of our teen's success, we are helping them to be aware of the feeling of accomplishment and self-worth.

This skill will also serve them when dealing with their peers. There will be times when our young adult will need to decide whether to "go with the pack" or make his own choices. Knowing that he does not need others to validate his decisions may make him stronger in resisting peer pressure.

If we assume that they won't remember basic skills, such as "brush your teeth," "make your lunch," or "have enough gas or cash," we are saying that we don't trust him to be independent enough to function on his own. A teen who feels trusted by an adult will feel proud and strive to live up to that trust.

We need to be on the lookout for good deeds, including great choices, smart ideas, extra efforts, helpfulness, examples of independence, acts of thoughtfulness, and newly acquired skills. We need to acknowledge our teen's efforts and their process as much as the outcome of their actions.

Be Real and Specific

It is important not to make things up. Find something that has actually happened and point out what in particular is meaningful. Our teens are smart enough to know the difference.

Here are some examples of specific praise:

- "I like the way you helped your sister this morning."
- "That is a great outfit. It looks sharp and should keep you warm."
- "You spent a long time cleaning your room. It looks so well organized."
- "You have been working on that science project for a long time. The detail is impressive."
- "Thanks for loading the dishwasher. It made my morning much easier."

We need to value our teen for who he is and praise him for what he has done. When he knows he has our respect, we are developing a powerful building block. *Recognition is a positive motivator.* All it takes is one small comment to make our teen's day.

It is a well-known secret that our teens don't always want us to know that our positive comments mean that much to them. Often, they keep a straight face or even shrug off our comments, but positive words land on their hearts and stick like glue. Unfortunately, negative comments do the same thing, and that's why we need to try hard to notice and comment on every positive act we can possibly acknowledge.

Sometimes, we might have to work hard to find a positive statement by catching them in a "moment of cooperation." Our teen may need to be reminded that she can do a task well.

When we see a glimpse of the behavior for which we are hoping, grab it, identify it, and mention it. We can say, "Thanks for catching the door so I did not have to put my bags down" or "Thanks for sliding over and sharing your seat." We need to be on patrol for the smallest hint of behavior that we can recognize, compliment, and encourage.

Use Constructive Criticism

Constructive criticism can be a valuable tool when raising our teens, but how and when we use criticism is also important. It is too easy to focus on what wasn't done well. Whenever possible, we should share five positives for each negative. A spoon full of sugar always helps get our message across!

Dad: When you cleaned out the garage, you didn't put the tools back in the right place.

or:

Dad: Thanks for cleaning out the garage, Steven. It is a dirty job and I have not been able to get to it for a while. It is so nice to walk in there and have it organized and swept up. I noticed that the tools were in a different place. I like to keep them on the shelf by the workbench. It is easier for me to find what I need when they are close by. Hey, I noticed that you rearranged the recycling bins. They look great!

In the second example, above, Dad made sure that he had lots of positive observations to go along with constructive criticism. Additionally, Dad did not blame Steven for the shortfall. Instead, he explained why one way worked better for him than another way. *Dad took the "right or wrong" judgment out of his remarks.*

Sean and Mom haven't gotten along in quite a while. Mom feels that Sean doesn't pick up after himself, doesn't do his chores, and spends as little time at home as possible. Most of their conversations come across as Mom nagging Sean and Sean blowing her off. Sean feels that, no matter what he does, it is not good enough for his mom, and that all she does is criticize him for what he doesn't do.

Mom: Did you take the trash out?

Sean: I forgot.

Mom: Well, when you take it out, could you also bring in the mail?

Sean: Sure.

Mom: So how was school? Did you get that test back?

Sean: It was okay. I got a C+.

Mom: Sean, you know that you have to do better than that! Cs aren't going to get you into a good college

Sean: Do you think that I don't know that?

Mom: Sean, don't be fresh.

Sean: Do you think that I don't care about my grades?

Mom: Well, it certainly doesn't seem to me that you do. You know that you can do better.

Sean: Sometimes it's just hard.

Mom: So ask for help. How come you won't talk to your teacher? Your teacher would definitely help. You just have to ask her.

Sean: Whatever, Mom.

Mom: Just go do the garbage like I asked.

Mom and Sean's conversation is painful for both of them. Mom is forgetting that part of her job—the fun part—is to notice the things that Sean is doing well:

- He is willing to be reminded to take out the trash.
- He will bring in the mail.
- He admits that he needs to do better in school.
- He tells her that he cares about his grades.

Mom missed an opportunity to glue some self-esteem onto her son's self-image by noticing that he can be cooperative, that he can be agreeable, and that he wants to do better.

Constructive criticism is different than negative thinking about our teen. If we catch ourselves saying, "He can't do anything right. He's a walking disaster," then we can force ourselves to find five things a day that he does right:

1. Did he clear his breakfast bowl?

2. Did he say something nice to his brother?

3. Did he hold the door for his sister?

4. Did he smile?

5. Did he take out the trash?

We can begin to share these observations with our teen. Acknowledge the good behavior, however minor it may be. It is a step in the right direction.

Mom and Sean can begin to think about each other differently because Mom has begun to notice the little things Sean is doing that come under the heading of good, kind, polite, cooperative, and considerate. Sean will begin to notice that Mom is appreciating him for something ... and a new cycle will begin.

While it is important for each of us to be able to hear and understand constructive criticism, it is also important for us to feel appreciated and valued for what we do contribute. *A kid who feels appreciated and valued has more self-esteem, and that characteristic will work like glue to keep him from falling apart when he goes through rough times.*

Use Encouragement

Praise usually follows an achievement or success, but we can give our teens encouragement even when they are not completely successful. *Encouragement focuses on strengths*, so teens can recognize their abilities and learn to feel confident and productive. We all need to learn to do things well. Teaching and learning tend to be more productive when done in a positive manner.

We can offer encouragement in many ways:

- Show faith.

- Give trust.

- Offer respect.

- Avoid comparisons.

- Recognize effort.

- Notice improvement.

- Be engaged.
- Focus on strengths and assets.

In the previous dialogue, Dad found a way to talk about what Steven did well in addition to what he did not do well. Dad emphasized that the *process* of Steven applying himself is as valuable as the *result*. This will help Steven to manage himself better, find internal approval, and acquire the ability to recognize his own efforts. This method will help him establish a stronger self-image.

Parents build self-esteem in advance. We start in childhood by saying "Good job!" to the toddler who falls and picks himself up. We invest in our teen's sense of self to enable him to stand up to peer pressure. We feed his confidence and inner strength to follow his own convictions when situations tempt him to do otherwise.

We have heard the adage, "We learn more from our failures than from our successes." There are many learning opportunities when our teen doesn't get it completely right. Using both encouragement and constructive criticism can be very productive. Remember to *recognize the learning process as well at the outcome.*

Steven: I'm never going to try to fix my car again! It is more messed up now than it was before!

Dad: Wow, this garage is trashed!

Steven: Gee, thanks a lot, Dad.

Dad: Come on, Steve. Where's your sense of humor? Show me what you have done. Perhaps we can figure some of this out together.

Dad tried to use humor, but Steven was not amused. Later, Dad came back with an observation that takes into account his son's process.

Dad: Steven, you really put a lot of effort into this. It may look like a mess, but you were able to figure out a few things. Perhaps you have realized that some problems require a professional.

Steven: But now the car and the garage are a mess!

Dad: Yes, I know. My mom used to say that you "can't make an omelet without breaking eggs." You had to take the car apart to see what was broken!

Teach Self-reliance

Self-reliance grows into self-confidence, which is part of strong self-esteem. *We should strive not to overprotect or pamper our teen while encountering life's ups and downs.* Our restraint leads to their ability to sharpen their problem-solving skills.

Teens need to develop a sense of self-sufficiency and accomplishment. We need to teach kids self-care skills and assign household chores. This allows our children to connect to a larger "group" and feel like a productive member. Don't do for teens what they can manage for themselves.

Waking teens up or reminding them that they have an appointment when they have a watch or clock is not helpful. Regularly searching for items our teen has misplaced, "snoopervising" homework, making money available whenever they need it, or planning their activities and coordinating their social schedule don't help either. We need to allow them to self-manage or they will feel incompetent. *We can't grow self-reliance or self-esteem from incompetency.*

- Self-esteem is the courage to be ourselves, to know who we are, and to like who we are. It is the beginning of practicing common sense and applying knowledge of ourselves and of others.
- Self-confidence is realizing that we can trust ourselves.
- Self-reliance is being grounded in independence and having the ability to solve problems.

Ideally, if we can help our teen manage their time, think wisely, take risks, and solve problems, they will develop self-reliance, which will breed self-confidence. *It all starts with knowing that they are good at something.* No matter how small of an accomplishment we can find, we should acknowledge it.

Dad: Steven, you weren't able to fix the car, but you had the guts to try. It takes courage to tackle problems under the hood. Clearly, by attempting this repair, you are learning more about engines. When we bring the car to the mechanic, we can ask him to explain this diagnosis so we can learn how to repair it for ourselves the next time. Who knows, maybe you can help us all figure out the issue behind the rattle in Mom's car!

Dad is helping Steven recognize his own value in the same way that we need to find ways to value our teen. We can let him know that we realize he is good at certain things, and then ask for help using his skills. We can say something like, "You are so clever with—. Can you help me figure this out?"

We can verbalize that we enjoy spending time with him by saying, "I had fun with you today." We can tell him that we like his ideas and suggestions, and compliment his clothing. This can be done in small doses. We are on patrol for the smallest pieces of behavior that we can recognize, compliment, and encourage.

It is important to identify when our teen is successful and "remind" her how she met that challenge. This will give her an opportunity to reflect and figure out for herself what she did that "worked."

For example, we might notice that our teen navigated a tough day. Perhaps she had a fight with her boyfriend or a misunderstanding with a teacher, or was laid off from a part-time job. In the past, she might have become totally frustrated and had a complete meltdown; this time, she did not.

Mom: Kelsey, I know you had a very tough day. I have seen that look in your eyes before, and it can mean that you are about to blow your lid, but you didn't. I know that you don't like losing it, but sometimes things just become too much. You were different this time. You stayed in control.

Kelsey: No big deal, Mom. I just didn't get that mad.

Mom: But that *is* a big deal. There have been times when you would get even madder because you didn't like the feeling of being really mad. This time you kept your cool.

Kelsey: Yeah, I can get pretty pissed off!

Mom: Something was different this time. What did you do or think that made your reaction change?

Kelsey: I didn't "do" anything on purpose. It's not like I planned it.

Mom: Think about it for a minute because, whatever you "happened" to do, it really helped. You stayed calm. It must have felt better not to blow up.

Kelsey: I guess I was a little different. I was mad at Dave. He really embarrassed me, but I remembered that he got in a fight with his mom last night. Even though I don't want him to treat me like that, I realized that he might be upset about something else. So I just went to my room and listened to my music.

Mom: Well, I think it is cool that you figured out how to keep it together.

It is enough for Kelsey to know that her mom noticed her coping behavior. Perhaps it is new for Kelsey to be able to use music to handle stress. Even if there is more to it than her daughter is able to explain, Mom has been able to focus attention on a success.

Anticipate Failures

It is important to understand that failure is a significant part of our teen's learning and growing experience. *We should not deny them the experience of failure because it is a way to learn, and it will make them stronger, smarter, and more resourceful.* Nevertheless, watching our teens fail or struggle is certainly one of the hardest things for us to do.

Here are some guidelines when failures occur for our teens:

- Don't tell her that she did a "fine" job when she did not.

- Try not to make excuses for her failure by blaming the teacher, boss, referee, or coach. She needs to learn how to be responsible for her own actions.

- Be understanding at the right time. The best time to offer our understanding is usually not right after a disappointment; sometimes it is best to wait an hour or two before we say anything. Disappointment is going to happen. If she earned it, let her feel it. The goal is to deal with it appropriately.

- Be supportive. Take the time to understand what she is feeling. Tell her that it is understandable that she feels this way, and that emotions are not always rational.

- Remind her of other important things in her life that have not changed. We can tell her that we love her no matter what. When the situation is more settled, we can help her learn from the mistake.

- Allow her to see that failure is an opportunity to do it differently next time. Tell her that we often build success and achievement on a series of mistakes. Ask her what she might do differently next time. Help her to learn from her mistakes and setbacks, which is a valuable life-coping skill.

Keeping mistakes and failures in perspective is another form of emotional literacy (see "Stability: Encouraging Emotional Literacy," in Chapter 4, "The Level"). If we can contain negative thoughts and events, they are less likely to snowball into other issues.

Mistakes do not have to define who we are. Losing a game doesn't make us a loser and failing a test doesn't make us a failure. Mistakes are a chance to learn. Mistakes can happen at school, at home, at work, and with friends. The key is to find the lesson for improvement and move on to the next challenge.

Inspire without Pressure

We need to challenge our teen but not threaten them. When we want our teen to strive for something new, challenge them. Encourage them to "go for it," and let them know that we support them. *A challenge is a positive way to engage with our teens.* It helps nurture their self-esteem.

Pressure or threats often come across as negative and could potentially diminish their self-esteem. Ideally, we want to inspire our teen to work hard and take on a new challenge. When we inspire them, we are positive and supportive, and help them set a realistic goal.

Here's an example of a threat versus a challenge:

- *Threat:* "If you can't pull yourself together, then you can't go."
- *Challenge:* "See if you can figure out what you need to do to make this happen. What do you need to do first?"

Goals and dreams are about results. They are helpful motivations and can guide us in the right direction. Goals help us to persevere, especially when the going gets tough, by giving us the focus to pull ourselves up after a fall. Steven's Dad did this when he suggested that Steven might learn more about fixing cars by watching the mechanic fix his, and he envisions Steven helping him fix Mom's car.

We want our teen to have the ability to self-manage, and to have the confidence to take healthy risks, make good choices, and solve problems—all of which will help lead our teen to feeling capable. If our teens can approach future challenges and opportunities feeling "up to the task," then they are off to a great start.

By giving responsibility, showing appreciation, and accepting mistakes, we are giving our teens the basic building blocks for a strong sense of self. Recognize that our teen's achievements and efforts are important pieces towards creating positive self-esteem.

Find ways to give them responsibility. Express appreciation for their efforts and accomplishments. Compliment her when she is being good at school or athletics, or when she has a clever idea or a sense of humor. Ask for her opinions and help. Accept her mistakes.

Be real, honest, and truthful. False praise and over-the-top congratulations can backfire. Our teen needs to believe that what we are saying is real and merited. Our teen will learn to self-manage and have the confidence to take healthy risks, make choices, and solve problems.

CHAPTER 10

Tricks of the Trade

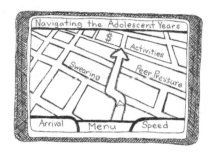

Tips to Help Navigate the Adolescent Years

This chapter will explore applications and uses of our tools with these common issues:

- Recognizing peer pressure

- Using code phrases

- Understanding swearing

- Discussing money issues

- Encouraging physical activity and special interests

Recognizing Peer Pressure

Peer pressure frightens many of us because it spotlights our teen's movement away from our influence. We worry about a variety of issues, including sex, alcohol, drugs, cigarettes, shoplifting, bullying, and cheating.

As friends and popular culture affect how our teens spend their time and the processes by which they make choices, we can feel powerless. We become concerned with the ways our teen will manage these added pressures.

Self-esteem (as discussed in Chapter 9, "The Glue") is an essential tool for our teens to help them navigate these new challenges. We should help them be aware that peer pressure comes in many forms, such as:

- The overt bully's threat: "Do it or else!"

- The teasing peer's threat: "What are you, chicken?"

- The covert friend's encouragement: "Come on! You'll like it. It'll be fun!"

A good place to begin teaching our teen about peer pressure is to provide specific information, which will help them have the data to make intelligent and safe decisions. Talking about consequences can take on a new meaning when we discuss peer pressure. Our tools (see "Discipline: Lefty Lucy, Righty Tighty" in Chapter 8, "The Screwdriver") will also be helpful.

We need to be clear about our positions and set explicit expectations. Acknowledge that it won't always be easy for our teens to stick to their decisions and opinions.

Peer pressure is not an excuse for bad behavior or poor choices; however, it *can* be a way of understanding how our teen got off track. We can also gain insight into a more appropriate response. We need to recognize the power that a peer group wields. We can begin by finding a quiet moment to talk.

Dad: John, do you have a few minutes?

John: Sure, Dad. What's up?

Dad: I know that this may sound lame, but I'd like to talk about peer pressure.

John: Are you for real? I'm 16, Dad. No one is going to bully me!

Dad: I believe that, but sometimes things aren't so obvious. Remember when the guys wanted to go camping on the beach, and you didn't really want to go but did anyway?

John: Yeah.

Dad: Well, you gave in to the group. Sometimes that is not a big deal; other times, it can be, and you end up doing something that you don't want to do.

It is important for us to help our teen recognize the potential influence of a friend or a group, and how important it is to identify their comfort level with the situation at hand. Showing that we, as parents, understand what it is like to "get swept along" in a moment can be valuable.

We want our teens to respect us and do what we ask, and we enjoy when they want to please us. Yet, if our teen is always striving to live up to parents' or teachers' expectations, then *the pattern is set for peer expectation and acceptance.* Learning that he or she can make a choice that another does not like, and still have unconditional regard, is crucial.

Using Code Phrases

There will be occasions when our teen is invited to do something that he feels is not a good idea but doesn't want to say no. It may be helpful to have a code phrase, which will let us know that he needs our help to decline.

For example, Phoebe is calling Mom on the phone and using the code of "asking for permission."

Phoebe: Hey, Mom. It's Phoebe. The kids are all going to Lisa's for a sleepover. Can I have permission to go, too? I'd really like to go.

Hearing the code, Mom responds:

Mom: I don't think so, Phoebe. I really need you to be home. Your Aunt Martha is coming over and she hasn't seen you in months.

Phoebe: Aunt Martha! She drives me crazy! Do I *have* to?

Mom: Yes, it is important.

Phoebe: Whatever. Okay, I'll be home soon.

Phoebe used the word "permission" in her request, which is a signal that Phoebe really does not want to go to Lisa's house and needs her mom to give her an out. Mom gets to play the bad guy, and Phoebe has "saved face" with her friends. Phoebe can hang up the phone and complain about her mom to all of her friends ... but then come home.

Understanding Swearing

Language is a big issue for many adults. Teens can achieve quite a reaction by their choice of words. Even permissive and relaxed parents have a threshold when it comes to certain types of language. Gone are the days of washing a kid's mouth out with soap when they swear, but the problem of inappropriate language still exists.

There are usually several factors at play when swearing becomes an issue. It is worthwhile to examine the context of the swearing:

- Are teens swearing around their friends to show off?
- Are swear words used as a sign of disrespect for parents or teachers?
- Are teens showing exasperation or being hurtful to others?
- Are they seeking attention?
- Is emotional illiteracy a factor? Remember: Not being able to express ourselves adequately can often result in falling back on standard phrases for anger or frustration.

There are several approaches to consider, depending on the source of the swearing. It is important that we watch our language; we should avoid using words that we do not want our teens to use. Make it clear what words are inappropriate or unacceptable. Understanding what the words actually mean can be eye opening to a teen.

Talk about why we will not tolerate certain words:

- Do they hurt feelings?
- Do they cause embarrassment?
- Are they disrespectful, vulgar, racist, or sexist?

Swearing often comes from not being able to express what we are actually feeling and then relying or falling back on vulgarities. Review the words in the "Words for Feelings" lists as well as the chart entitled "How Do You Feel Today?" (Chapter 4, "The Level"). *When we can better figure out what we are feeling, we can communicate more effectively by choosing better words.*

It may also be motivating to look at how Shakespeare used words to insult others. It's unlikely that our teens will quote Shakespeare when they are angry, but it is a good illustration of how nondescript most swearing is. Shakespeare offers examples (many of which can be found on t-shirts, coffee mugs, and posters) that model insulting perfectly.

Here are some examples:

- "All eyes and no sight."
- "You are a lump of foul deformity."
- "I do desire we may be better strangers."
- "There's no more faith in thee than in a stewed prune."
- "You are as a candle, the better burnt out."
- "Foot Licker!"
- "You are such a puppet."
- "Do you worship idiots?"
- "You are an infectious pest!"
- "Are you a mindless slave?"
- "You remorseless, treacherous, lecherous villain!"

Discussing Money Issues

We need to talk to our teens about money. We carve out time to discuss dating and drugs, but rarely do we discuss money. The tools discussed in "Having, Losing, and Regaining Trust" (Chapter 7, "The Measuring Tape") and "Self-esteem and Self-confidence: The Stuff That Holds It All Together" (Chapter 9, "The Glue") can be used here as well.

We don't want our teens to worry about money, but we do want them to manage their money, understand its value, and spend it wisely. Budgeting, saving, and learning how to choose what we buy and when to buy something are significant life skills. These transitional years are a great time to help our teens learn sound money-management skills.

Money is more abstract than it used to be due to credit and debit cards, automatic teller machines, and checks. Teens may notice that sometimes we use a credit card and other times we use cash. They have watched us push ATM buttons to make money "magically" appear.

We can talk with our teen about money on an adult level. Introduce the concept of providing for basic needs (e.g., food, clothing, shelter, education, and transportation). Next, begin setting priorities on what our teen wants to buy. Life is about realistic choices. Discussing the motivation for a purchase is a good way to begin the conversation because it builds on the idea of emotional literacy.

Having an impulsive desire is not always a bad thing, but we need to be aware of our reasons for buying an item. *Determining whether something is a "need" or a "want" is important information.* Pose questions that will cause our teen to consider why they want to make a specific purchase, and contrast that with other choices they might have made. They will learn to ask themselves, "Is this a want, a need, or an impulse purchase?"

Whether it is $50 for a video game or $100 for sneakers, ask our teen to figure out:

- How long would it take to earn that money?

- How many uses can she expect to get out of the purchase?

- Is the item worth it?

For example, if a shirt costs $48, and she thinks she will wear it once a week for the summer, have her do the math: 48 divided by 12 = $4 per wear. Perhaps she'll only wear it six times, so now it's $8 per wear. Maybe she wants to buy a $60 swimsuit, which she will wear several times a week. The cost per use might be less then $2 per wear.

Sometimes we can ask our teen to choose one item they want from several choices. Help them put it in perspective:

- What would she give up to acquire this? If we know that she has been hoping for a new iPod, we can point out that this purchase delays the new iPod.

- If a teen has a job for $8 per hour, what is the cost ratio of the purchase? Is it worth three hours of babysitting, waitressing, or lawn mowing?

We can model the decision process for our teens. Don't say, "We can't afford it" if it's not true. Instead, take the time to explain: "We're saving for college (or a vacation or a new car)." It may help to qualify this choice by explaining the rationale behind it: "We think that this is more important because ..." Our teens will learn from watching us make choices.

Finding the opportunity to teach our teen the value of financial responsibility is a win-win situation. We may want to consider introducing them to debit or prepaid cards, which can provide hands-on experience without finance charges. Actually, cards can be safer than cash because a cardholder is usually not liable for a stolen card or an unauthorized purchase. Most banks grant the parent the ability to monitor purchases and set up automatic spending limits. *Educating our teen today means a more financially equipped adult tomorrow.*

Involve kids in charitable donations. One family I know gives each child an amount of money at Christmas to donate to a charity of their choice. The amount could be $5 or $500. The amount is less important than the awareness and the action. Each child researched a charity, made a choice, and explained why. The child then took the money to the charity and personally donated it.

Whether from a part-time job, gifts, or an allowance, when teens have their own money, they are more likely to appreciate its value. Teens should save a minimum of 10% to 20% of their earnings. Show them a compound interest chart, so they can visualize the power and magnitude of saving:

Compound Interest Tables: The Value of $1,000 Invested in a Lump Sum

	4%	8%	12%	16%
10 Years	$1,480	$2,158	$3,105	$4,411
20 Years	$2,191	$4,661	$9,646	$19,460
30 Years	$3,243	$10,062	$2,9960	$85,850
40 Years	$4,801	$21,724	$93,051	$378,721
50 Years	$7,106	$46,901	$289,002	$1,670,703

Whether they are saving $10 a week, $100 a month, or $1,000 a year, it is important for them to learn the power of saving.

Encouraging Physical Activity and Special Interests

We take a nonnegotiable position on teeth brushing, bathing, wearing seatbelts, not swimming alone, or playing near high-traffic roads. We can also be firm about good eating habits, physical activity, and the development of special interests.

Culturally, as we strive for contentment, we have come to recognize the importance of balance. Many of us have grown up with the mantra "Work hard and play hard," which implies—to us and to our teens—that we need to have a variety of things in our lives.

Teens who are active and develop personal hobbies build self-esteem. A sense of accomplishment, independence, and self-reliance are integral parts in becoming successful teens and, ultimately, successful adults. Encouraging and establishing a passion for an activity can be the counterweight that keeps a teen from straying off course.

- A person who loves an activity, like tennis or soccer, is more likely to take better care of themselves because they need their body to be in good shape.

- A person who loves horses or dogs will grow an appreciation for taking care of the well-being of an animal.

- A person who paints or builds is less apt to be "hanging around with nothing to do."

This is another great opportunity to lead by example. Kids need to see that we believe it's important to be healthy and take care of ourselves. Being fit and having a hobby is also a chance to share outings and interests with them. As parents, teachers, and mentors, we can be firm about "requiring" that our kids have multiple interests. This is a great way to introduce the goal of striving for our personal best.

Not everything needs to be a competition or even have a sports focus. Find alternatives, such as martial arts, hiking, hip-hop or other forms of dancing, bike riding, yoga, and walking.

Many families joke about "Forced Family Fun"; sometimes we just need to get out there and do something! Don't be nervous about trying something new or being a little silly. Our teens may complain about having to spend time with us, but we may be surprised by how much we (and they) enjoy it!

CHAPTER 11

Voltage Meter

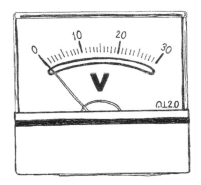

Warning Signs: Danger! *Danger!*

A voltage meter lets us know the heat level or the level of danger of a situation. There comes a time when we need to recognize that a situation is more serious than we thought, or has escalated beyond our ability to handle it on our own.

While the focus of *The Tool Box* has been the mainstream teen, we also need to acknowledge that some teens will have "diagnosable" issues, such as:

- Attention deficit hyperactivity disorder
- Attention deficit disorder
- Obsessive-compulsive disorder
- Oppositional defiant disorder
- Eating disorders

- Learning disabilities
- Processing disorders
- Substance abuse

It seems appropriate to spend some time outlining the warning signs of real trouble because sometimes we may not be able to fully comprehend that our teen has crossed the line into a danger zone. We need to be ready to notice when a different set of challenges may be looming on the horizon, including drugs and alcohol, eating disorders, and depression.

Here are some warning signs that we can use to help determine if our teen is heading for serious trouble:

- Loss of interest in hobbies, sports, or other favorite activities
- Atypical energy display
- Unreliability, such as skipping school, missing work, and breaking commitments
- Abrupt changes in relationships, such as replacing old friends with new ones
- Rapid, obsessive speech
- Agitation and fidgeting
- Irritability
- Difficulty sleeping
- Changes in sleeping patterns, such as sleeping at odd times
- Nightmares
- Appetite disturbance with weight change
- Restlessness
- Decreased or low energy
- Memory loss
- Feelings of worthlessness
- Feelings of guilt
- Intense fear and helplessness
- Difficulty concentrating and unclear thinking
- Paranoid behavior

- Delusions and hallucinations
- Suicidal thoughts or words
- Truancy
- Impulsive and risky choices
- Declining school grades
- Physical injuries that don't make sense
- Carelessness about appearance
- Extreme mood shifts
- Self-isolation
- Bursts of unexplained anger
- Violent threats toward siblings or parents
- Not coming home

Drugs and Alcohol

Our teens will face important decisions of whether to use psychoactive drugs (i.e., drugs that affect the mind and emotion), such as alcohol, marijuana, cocaine, narcotics, and methamphetamines. There are also socially acceptable drugs, including caffeine, nicotine, ibuprofen, and antihistamines, as well as prescription drugs, such as antibiotics, antidepressants, attention deficit meds, sleeping aids, and tranquilizers.

We live in a culture that is not always clear about what is and is not acceptable. These boundaries vary from family to family and among social groups. Our teens deal with this "mixed message" daily, so we need to be as clear as possible about our own expectations. For more information, visit www.drugfree.org.

There may be a problem if the following behavioral signs exist:

- Rapid mood swings, such as from euphoria to depression, or from withdrawal to hostility
- Withdrawal from family activities, meals, and celebrations
- New friends who refuse to meet parents
- Inability to follow family rules, complete homework, or keep appointments

- Change in personality, such as from energetic and outgoing to depressed and noncommunicative, or when a shy, quiet teen becomes overly outgoing

- Shift of blame to others and deflection of consequences to the point of feeling persecuted or paranoid

- Happy, depressed, hostile, or angry moods for no apparent reason

- Self-absorbed behavior

- Unwillingness to discuss important issues

- Display of radically new clothing or hair

- Increase in school problems

- Compulsive talkativeness

- Jittery body movements

- Weight gain or loss

- Fatigue

- Shaky hands

- Dizzy spells

- Chronically inflamed nostrils and/or a runny nose

For more information, visit www.abovetheinfluence.com.

Eating Disorders

We all need food to survive, although we eat for many different reasons. Sometimes we are hungry; sometimes our friends are eating; perhaps something just looks too yummy to pass up. Meals tend to punctuate our days. There are times when we reward ourselves with a favorite food when we have accomplished a task or when we have come through a tough time.

Sometimes eating—or not eating—becomes an addiction or an obsession. When people who are trying to lose weight surround us, body image can become a crushing influence. Teens that develop eating disorders are often bright, talented, and competent, and present a confident façade to the world around them.

An eating disorder can last a few months or a lifetime. Many people do not recognize how dangerous eating disorders can be. They can hijack a person's life, leaving ruined relationships, lost opportunities, illness, and depression in their wake. Anemia, cardiac arrest, a ruptured esophagus, amenorrhea (i.e., the absence of a menstrual period), infertility, and kidney, liver, and heart damage are common consequences. *Eating disorders can be deadly.*

There are three main types of eating disorders:

- *Anorexia nervosa* is a type of self-starvation. It can start out as a dieting plan, which slides into dangerous territory. Anorexia depletes the body of nutrients, muscles deteriorate, and minerals are sucked from bones. As bodily protein deteriorates, hair and nails become brittle, dull, thin, and broken. Hair may fall out and skin becomes pale and dry.

- *Bulimia nervosa* includes binge eating and purging. People will eat huge quantities of food, and then vomit or use laxatives to expel that food. Compulsive exercising is also common. Bulimics may seem to be an average weight, but the physical stress from purging on their body is destructive. Repeated vomiting includes damaging the bile ducts and overstimulating stomach acids, which can scar the esophagus, mouth, and teeth. Habitual use of laxatives can cause bowel dysfunction and colon ulcers.

- *Compulsive overeating* and *obesity* often go hand in hand, and each puts a tremendous strain on our bodies. These eating disorders can cause high blood pressure, osteoarthritis, heart disease, gall bladder disease, and diabetes. People can suffer from a combination of two or more disorders.

Here are some typical signs of eating disorders:

- Yellowing and/or deterioration of the teeth

- Sore throat

- Scar or sore on the index or middle finger (made by stomach acids from constantly inducing vomiting)

- Lack of energy

- Dramatic weight loss

- Constipation

- Avoidance of family meals

- Excess hair on face and body

- Hair loss

- Loss of menstrual cycle
- Fainting spells
- Sleep difficulties
- Eating rituals, such as eating certain foods or eating them in a specific order
- Food restrictions

For more information, visit www.eatingdisordershelpguide.com.

Depression

There maybe times when our teen just can't shake off his negative emotions and thoughts, when he feels that he has made a terrible mistake, or when things happen that upset his life. Perhaps he cannot imagine feeling happy again. This may last a few days or even a week, and eventually he manages to snap out of it; however, there may be times when he might not snap back so easily.

When negative feelings turn into hopelessness, and when that hopelessness continues for weeks or months, he might be experiencing depression. If depression lasts long enough for him to lose interest in people and things around him, this is a concern and a signal for help.

Here are some typical signs of depression:

- Change in eating and sleeping habits
- Loss of interest in friends or hobbies
- Suddenly not caring for pets or prized possessions
- Sudden change in school grades
- Withdrawal
- Lack of interest in appearance
- Difficulty thinking
- Hopelessness or feelings of self-hate
- Numb, uninterested, or listless feelings
- Loss of energy
- Talk of thoughts about death and dying

For more information, visit www.teendepression.org.

Suicide

At some point, many of us may have thought, "I wish I were dead." Most often, we don't actually *mean* that we wish were dead; instead, we mean that we want relief from a situation.

There are many reasons why people might consider suicide: ending a relationship, feeling helpless in a situation, getting cut from a team, not getting a part in the play, or losing someone or something special. There is an intense feeling of being overwhelmed, a sense of deep loss, and a feeling that there is no way out of the current dilemma.

Here are some signs of suicidal behavior:

- Major personality changes
- Decreased appetite
- Self-destructive behavior
- Change in sleep patterns
- Change in friends and social activities
- Prized possession distribution to others
- Preoccupation with death
- Obsessive fear of world destruction
- Overwhelming guilt or shame
- Talk about suicide, particularly with a specific plan
- Access to drugs or weapons
- After a long depression or withdrawal, a shift to an unexplainable peacefulness or an unusual cheerfulness that everything is now great

Certainly, we could consider many of these signs as being within the realm of "normal" teenage behavior. *It is not always easy to determine when our teen may have wandered into dangerous territory.*

It is important that we stay aware and tuned in. If we get a sense that things might be off track, it is time to contact a professional for specific advice and help, such as a family doctor, minister, rabbi, or therapist.

For more information, visit www.helpguide.org/mental/depression_teen. htm.

CHAPTER 12

Building a Tool Belt

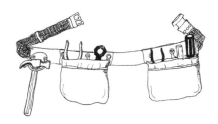

Helping our Teen Build a Set of Useful Tools

In this book, we have discussed several tools that we can use with our teens. Another application for this information is to help build a Tool Belt for them. The metaphor of a Tool Belt can be helpful. Having a visual image of a concept or process often puts things in perspective. Nailing a nail without a hammer is challenging!

Kids are hungry for ways to make things work better and to have things go more easily and smoothly in their lives. This is what a tool does. Think about what our teen—as well as our younger children—need to get the job, challenge, or issue resolved. This concept is similar to the box of crayons that we talked about in "Stability: Encouraging Emotional Literacy" (Chapter 4, "The Level"). Don't give them more than they can handle, but do give them the tools they need.

Here are a few suggestions for the Tool Belt. Some are variations of tools we have already discussed, and some are new concepts specifically for our teen.

ABCs (Ask, Brainstorm, Choose, Do, and Evaluate)

This is a great sequence for our teens to use in many situations that involve problem solving and compromise (see "Problem Solving and the Art of Compromise" in Chapter 6, "3-in-1 Oil").

Change It Up

This allows our teen to recognize that they can choose to respond differently to another person or situation. They will learn that they can only control their own actions, and they'll see that sometimes it is the best way to affect change in others (see "Change the Dance" in Chapter 2, "Opening the Toolbox").

Code Phrase

Giving our kids a code phrase to let us know that they want us to say no to their request can be extremely valuable. There are times when it is helpful to give our teen an "easy out" (see "Using Code Phrases" in Chapter 10, "Tricks of the Trade").

Hall Pass

A hall pass is giving someone permission to make an exception to a rule. Using a hall pass acknowledges that this is a special situation, which normally wouldn't happen.

HALT (Hungry / Angry / Lonely / Tired) and the Growing Box of Crayons

HALT is a great tool for our teens. Encourage them to think about their feelings using this acronym and be ready to introduce the fuller arrays of emotions as they mature (see Chapter 4, "The Level"). Like a box of colored crayons, our teens will learn to recognize a larger array of emotions within themselves when they need to express day-to-day situations and personal experiences in more detail.

Hazard Lights

We use hazard lights to warn other cars that there is danger ahead. Likewise, we can use "hazard lights" to show our teen that trouble might be headed their way. We can demonstrate to our teen how to step back and anticipate when and where there might be an issue or a challenge they will have to face. Perhaps it is midterm week, or a social gathering includes an old girlfriend or a situation with a conflict of interest. Being aware that there is potential for a problem will enable our teen to prepare himself. One of the worst kinds of trouble is "surprise" trouble. It is no big deal if it rains as long as we have an umbrella!

Litmus Paper

We can use litmus paper to determine the type of problem or situation with which we are dealing. We cannot control certain things, such as the weather, the economy, or school; however, we can control how we *react* to them. We have power over many things *within* our control. Once we figure out what these things are, we can come up with a plan of action. When our teens learn to recognize the scope of a situation, they are more apt to understand their own part in it (see "Think Globally Versus Locally" in Chapter 4, "The Level").

Mirror

A mirror reflects someone else's feelings or words. The skill of reflective listening comes in handy, and we can teach our teen how to use it. If a friend or teacher, for example, is angry about an issue, the teen can use a mirror to help reflect it back instead of becoming defensive by saying, "So, it sounds like you are angry because ..." ("Get Connected by Listening and Communicating" in Chapter 3, "Nuts and Bolts," offers further discussion about reflective listening.) Mirroring helps to provide clarity before a situation escalates.

Teflon Suit

Teflon is a coating for pots and pans, which keeps things from sticking to them. There are times when our teen needs to protect themselves, especially in sticky situations—perhaps a social situation that she knows is going to be challenging, or a negative scenario that she anticipates. If we are prepared for a situation, we can handle it better. When we are ready and equipped, we feel more competent in responding (discussed in Chapter 4, "The Level").

White Flags

White flags are used for irrational fears. We might intellectually *know* that something is true, fair, or accurate, but it is not how we *feel*. We know the world is not going to end because we failed an exam, lost a game, or didn't get a role in the play, but we feel like it will. Our teen can "wave the white flag," acknowledging that her feelings may not be rational but allowing that the emotions attached to them are very real. This lets us (and others) recognize that she needs to focus on the emotional—and not the rational—side of an event.

Let's Sum It Up

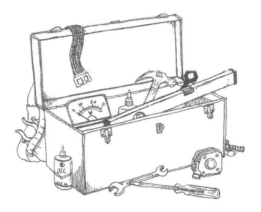

Using the Tool Box

There are no easy answers and no instruction manuals. There are no standard scripts to follow but rather guidelines and examples of real scenarios that can help provide a picture of how teen issues can be handled differently. *The Tool Box* offers an alternative approach. It demonstrates the importance of setting reasonable and clear goals while offering guidance, tools, and skills that make the process easier.

Success comes from understanding and trusting ourselves as well as understanding and trusting our teens. Respecting their likes and dislikes, and acknowledging their strengths and weaknesses, are good first steps. Treating our teens with respect and finding ways to show them our love and regard are equally important.

We all want to help our teens grow up with a strong sense of who they are and what they can achieve. The information in this book will enable them to handle life's challenges and discover more avenues for success.

Change is good. Change is healthy.

As with many projects, we can use one tool for several things, such as using the handle of a screwdriver for a crude hammer. The more comfortable we become with our tools, the more uses we will have for them. In a pinch, makeshift will work; however, for the long haul, it is best to get the right tool for the job.

Parenting is a challenge, whether it is the "terrible twos," potty training, or navigating the ever-changing waters of the teenage years. Maintaining our balance and focus as we strive to be clear and consistent with our teen is essential to success.

- *Listen.* Don't make everything a "life lesson." Let her talk it through, ask her questions, and let her contemplate different answers. Validate her frustration or anger and reflect her complicated range of emotions. Help her find the right words to describe what she is feeling. By listening first, we are able to have a fuller sense of what is "going on" with our teen, which gives us the opportunity to form a better response.

- *Catch them being good.* Even if only a small part of what we see is good, notice that part and comment on it.

- *Use conflict and compromise.* Apply the ABCs (**A**sk, **B**rainstorm, **C**hoose, **D**o, and **E**valuate) and carefully select the topics over which we choose to battle.

- *Change the dance.* Don't be afraid to try something different. If we are waltzing and it is not working, then it is time to tango!

- *Be specific about an issue.* Concentrate on one thing at a time. We need to have a specific example of our upset feelings so we can help our teen understand the issue. Don't bring up other issues. Stay focused.

- *Request changes in a positive way.* Find a kind way to ask them to do something. Note a positive aspect before we point out a negative one. Avoid put downs and name calling.

- *Expect disagreements.* This is a normal part of every relationship. Some disagreements are just miscommunications, which usually happen when someone is unclear about what is bothering them, hasn't said what they really mean, leaves out information and assumes it is already known, or brings up unresolved issues that are bubbling under the surface.

It is important to:

- *Practice trust.* Blend forgiveness and compassion with responsibility and clear boundaries.

- *Use discipline.* Consistency is vital. Connect consequences to the infraction. No one is perfect, so make sure that we create a path on which our teen can return.

- *Find time to be alone with them.* Let them know that they are important enough to make time just for them.

- *Keep cool.* Try not to respond with anger. Slow it down and listen. Figure out what is truly going on for the teen. If we wait until we have calmed down, it will have much more impact.

- *Model desired behavior.* Behave like the person we want them to be.

- *Share decision-making processes.* Help them understand "how" we come to conclusions.

- *Allow (or create) opportunities for self-responsibility.* This is so important in building strong self-esteem. Try not to overindulge. Doing too much for our teens is not helping them. They need to figure out how to navigate the system, whether it is making an appointment for a haircut or learning to make mac 'n cheese. With responsibility comes earned independence.

- *Set boundaries and expectations ahead of time.* This includes dating, work, schoolwork, alcohol, and drugs.

- *Find things to do together.* Some examples are yard work, housecleaning, car washing, dishwashing, preparing meals, watching movies, eating dinner, walking, playing sports and games, watching favorite TV shows, and listening to music and attending concerts.

- *Be polite.* Use manners, show respect, and be courteous to everyone.

- *Say something nice.* Let our teen know what we like about things they have done or how they have been acting. Spend as much time being positive as being negative.

- *Talk about our own day.* Let our teen know about our day, including the ups and downs. It is an easy way for them to feel included.

- *Ask their advice.* Everyone likes to feel appreciated and helpful. We may be surprised by their insights and observations.

- *Look for solutions.* Focus on moving forward. Figure out how we can alter the situation so that, in the future, we can hope for a new result. Blame makes finding new solutions harder, so invent ways to work together and navigate new situations.

- *Avoid swearing.* There are often better and more effective words we can use to make our point. Swearing tends to be hurtful and aggressive, which undermines true communication.

- *Be aware of barriers or challenges to good communication.* Ask questions and make sure that we have as much information and as many facts as possible.

- *Avoid distractions.* Put down the phone, turn off the TV, and resist multitasking. Give communication plenty of time—not when we have only 10 minutes before we have to go somewhere else.

Stop, look, and listen to our teen. If we let go of what we think "we know" about our teen, we will learn more about his world.

By developing a neutral approach, we will be more likely to hear and understand what is happening in a given circumstance. This act of understanding may unlock a difficult situation. Understanding is the beginning of communicating, and this will help us figure out new tools that we might try. Many things are in transition, and we need to be able to change and grow with them.

Please take this collection of tools, break them in, and test which ones feel good. Use them in different situations and see how they work. Talk about them and share them. The more we work with the tools, the more comfortable we will become with them. Remember to listen, find the right tool, and practice using it!

Even though parenting is challenging, with the right set of tools, we will find that we can enjoy the process!

Made in the USA
Middletown, DE
21 June 2018